AF413602

the CURRENCY *of* HEAVEN

The Currency of Heaven

How to Trust God for More Than Enough

Taylor A. Welch

Published by Game Changer Publishing

Paperback ISBN: 979-8-90158-000-4

Hardcover ISBN: 979-8-90158-001-1

Digital ISBN: 979-8-90158-002-8

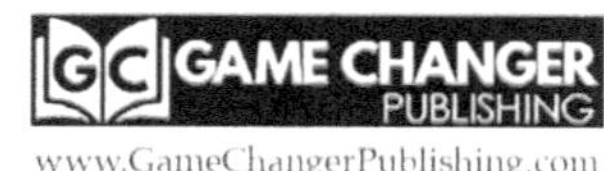

www.GameChangerPublishing.com

Dedicated to God's people—

*Even the ones who do not know it yet. We are all part
of a greater story than we could ever imagine.*

the
CURRENCY
of
HEAVEN

HOW TO TRUST GOD FOR MORE THAN ENOUGH

TAYLOR A. WELCH

ACKNOWLEDGMENTS

My wife, Lindsey: Thank you for showing me Jesus when I could not find Him. Thank you for choosing me when I did not know what it was like to be chosen. Thank you for never leaving when I was full of rejection and would have been easy to leave. Thank you for looking at me and actually seeing me. Thank you for believing when I did not believe, and for making sure I did not forget. Thank you for showing me the kingdom of heaven. No one outside of heaven will ever know how much you mean to me or how important you are.

Isi Igenegba: Thank you for teaching me how to pray, for showing me a "1 Corinthians 4:20" life, and making me go big or go home.

Dale Mast: Thank you for proving to me that the most important thing to know is what God thinks about me, and for speaking prophetically over me the things I would never have received from anybody else.

Jesus: Most of the stories in this book are about you. I have no idea why you would risk what you risked to get me back, but I will not waste it. Thank you for being real with me. I will not quit until you tell me to.

FOREWORD

I have come to see that there are two kinds of messages: those born out of study and those born out of encounter. This book is the latter. Like its author, it is forged in fire, matured through obedience, and written as a holy epistle for generations.

I have had the privilege of knowing Taylor as a brilliant mind and a man deeply committed to the integrity of kingdom patterns. As our paths cross at the intersection of prophetic governance and spiritual reformation, I have seen a man who doesn't just reach for truth but willingly lives under its weight as he blends strategy with surrender. Only such a man could have been trusted by Heaven to write about its currency.

As I went through the pages of this manuscript, every chapter felt like a summons forcing me to reconsider the heart and principles by which I have governed my life so far, tracing every transaction back to its altar. As you read, it is impossible to ignore the sacred provocation to reject the seductive voices of

Baal, Mammon, and performance and instead return to the purity of trust as Heaven's most valuable currency.

In my years of ministry, leadership, and spiritual governance across nations, I have seen firsthand the strongholds of fear, scarcity, and orphanhood that limit God's people. I have seen believers pray for abundance while still worshiping at the altar of anxiety. I have seen nations cry out for reformation while still measuring success by the metrics of Pharaoh, but this book interrupts it all. Every chapter is a gateway, ushering you into realities like:

- The anatomy of Baal's economic seduction
- The war over imagination and belief systems
- The power of altars in shaping financial outcomes
- The difference between trading with God versus manifesting with self
- How Heaven recognizes trust, not hustle

I can honestly say that there is an anointing upon these words, not for hype, but for the possibility of systemic revival and holy reconstructions. By the power of the Holy Spirit, you will see hidden idols in thought patterns that you thought were normal. You will be drawn back into the ancient pattern of Eden, where intimacy, obedience, and stewardship were the only currencies ever needed.

If you're tired of surviving on principles without presence, then do not skip a line in this book because this material is for anyone called to multiply resources without compromising their soul. It is for those who understand that financial deliverance begins with spiritual recalibration.

Taylor has written what many were afraid to say and what many have needed to hear. Just like Samson's foxes on fire, I see the words of this book breaking through the fields of systems and dismantling what culture has taught generations about wealth, worth, and worship. In God's mercy, through this book, we're given another chance to understand how obedience births increase, where generosity becomes warfare, and where trust becomes our most valuable asset.

To the reader:

I thought I was just reading a book, but as I journeyed deeper, I realised the holy inscriptions were also reading me; like a living, breathing entity, *The Currency of Heaven* carries an undeniable presence that compels you to pause, repent, and worship God! My advice to you is: let it break your old altars and install fresh divine instructions that will recalibrate your mind and prepare you to effectively occupy in these last days. I am confident that as you do this, you'll find yourself being slowly ushered into a life where Heaven can trust you with its resources. After all, why operate in deficit when you can run in the sufficiency of Zion?

Welcome to *The Currency of Heaven*.

—Apostle Isi Igenegba
Lead Pastor of the People of Influence Network and founder of the Isi Benedicta Institute

CONTENTS

INTRODUCTION

The human race was born into absolute prosperity. In the beginning, God placed Adam and Eve in the Garden of Eden and provided for every need. There was perfect balance. What we had was equal to everything we could ever want.

When sin entered the world, that provision was broken, and for the first time, humanity experienced "lack." Now we suffer the frustration of wanting *more* than we could have. The human brain has undergone many thousands of years of changes to defend itself from this unnatural experience called scarcity.

Research in evolutionary psychology suggests our brains have an ancestral expectation of sufficiency. They remember on some level that we were designed for abundance. As resources became harder to access, humans developed systems to manage this inherited scarcity.

Humanity turned to production as a way to get back to abundance. More labor, more innovation, more industry, all in a vain attempt to get back to something we already had. While our production capacity has increased exponentially, our ability to enjoy what we accumulate has remained static. The hedonic treadmill of greed, anxiety, and the endless pursuit of more has become a defining part of modern life. If you've ever felt like there is never enough, no matter what you do, this is why.

After helping more than 5,000 clients navigate the maze of wealth creation, I began to ask myself, *What is the point?* I have helped people get rich, but wealth alone does not prevent suffering. In fact, it sometimes seemed to invite it. People burn out, they get divorced, they lose loved ones, or lawsuits happen. As the saying goes, "More money, more problems."

Prosperity without a clear sense of purpose and identity can become its own form of imprisonment. If you reach the top without being ready for the top, you will give it all back. I have seen people achieve financial success, only to feel more lost, overwhelmed, or disconnected than before. I was helping people create financial windfalls, but something always seemed to be missing. I grew bitter. A few years ago, I decided I would either figure out why this kept happening or I would stop helping people create financial progress altogether. I began by looking objectively at my past. We are all a byproduct of our programming, but by whom and for what?

My professional life started in American megachurches. I spent years on staff or traveling with the teams of some of the largest congregations in the country. I noticed many Christians had distorted views of money and prosperity.

Most people's failures in this area are due to faulty programming. It's not that we want to lack; it's that we weren't taught how to get wealth the right way. We read the Bible and do not understand what it means. If we do not understand Scripture, we cannot properly obey it.

Approximately 15 percent of Jesus' recorded words focused on wealth, and his teachings consistently warn about placing money too high in the hierarchy of your life. He never takes a stance against abundance, but instead condemns resourcefulness divorced from wisdom.

LOST IN TRANSLATION

In the Gospel of Matthew, Jesus states, "No one can be a slave of two masters, since either he will hate one and love the other or be devoted to one and despise the other. You cannot be slaves of God and of money" (Matt. 6:24).

The Greek word translated as "slave" in this passage is *douleō* (δουλεύω). Unlike the English word "slave," which implies ownership or forced labor, *douleō* refers to an internal and often voluntary form of bondage. Jesus was not against having resources, but being enslaved to the pursuit of them.

Rejecting all wealth because of the potential danger is like abandoning automobiles because car accidents happen. The danger lies not in the tool, but in how we relate to it.

In 1 Timothy 6:10, Paul warns, "For the love of money is a root of all kinds of evils." The Greek word used here, philargyria (φιλαργυρία), refers to an obsessive or greedy attachment to money, rather than simple possession. The message, in layman's terms, is not to be obsessed with what you possess.

Modern psychological research affirms the validity of this wisdom. It is not the possession of wealth that damages us, but the compulsive pursuit of more. Studies have shown that materialism and the relentless quest for wealth are associated with lower life satisfaction and increased psychological distress.

The idea of wealth as both a blessing and a curse fits the definition of a paradox. A paradox is something that seems like a contradiction, but turns out to be true when you look more closely, and the Bible is absolutely full of them. If we don't take the time to understand both sides, we risk missing the wisdom that lies in the middle. Life exists in the grey spaces between extremes, and so does wisdom about wealth.

THE BATTLE OVER WEALTH

When an encamped army is guaranteed to lose, it often stops trying to achieve victory and refocuses on taking as many people down with them as they can. The goal is no longer to win the war, but to make the enemy's victory costly. Historians call this the Fabian strategy, named after the Roman General Fabian Maximus, who avoided direct confrontation with Hannibal and instead wore him down through delay and attrition.

For thousands of years, we've witnessed this strategy play out in the realm of the Spirit. The rules of engagement that power the cosmos prevent Satan from killing you directly. However, he can slow you down, confuse you, and reduce your capabilities until you are no longer able to accomplish your mission on Earth.

Most of what drives a person's life occurs in the spirit before we see it in the natural. In fact, anything you see in the physical is likely a manifestation of something operating on a spiritual level. Currency on Earth works similarly to currency in Heaven. You can save it, store it, multiply it, or squander it. Before we cover the concepts of wealth, greed, and poverty, we must understand why and how God orders these things.

This is not a book on financial management in the traditional sense. My goal is not to teach you how to earn, save, or invest better, but to show you why trusting His process is more important than chasing our own outcomes.

Your adversary has weaponized prosperity and poverty to take you away from your purpose, whether it is through distraction, anxiety, love of money, or an unhealthy fixation on poverty as a symbol of goodness. The enemy has installed a terrible dichotomy into our thinking, but he has lied. There is an interested God on the other side who wants to help you, protect you, and promote you.

It is not sufficient to understand only the spiritual principles. You must partner with what God wants to do through you by developing wisdom, discipline, and skill. This book will begin by helping you understand how spiritual systems work and then move into the practical mechanics of monetary multiplication.

DIVINE STRATEGY

 *"Then God said, 'Let us make human beings in our image, to be like us.'"*
—Genesis 1:26 (NLT)

Over the more than twenty years I have spent studying spiritual and economic principles, I have observed that many Christians hold a fundamentally flawed understanding of wealth and prosperity. From an early age, we are conditioned to fear something that is not only essential for survival but can also be a positive force when approached with the right intentions.

A comprehensive study of religious attitudes toward wealth conducted by Harvard Divinity School in 2022 found that Western Christian denominations exhibit significantly higher rates of what researchers term "prosperity anxiety."

The research is backed by the anecdotal experience of the several hundred thousand personal customers, students, and clients I have taught over the last ten years. In Christianity's well-intentioned efforts to inoculate people against greed, we have cultivated something equally destructive: generational poverty.

Biblical scholars note that the Hebrew word for poverty, rēš (רִישׁ)[1], appears in Scripture not as a virtue, but as a condition to be overcome through wisdom and divine guidance. The Bible consistently frames poverty as a hardship, not a spiritual ideal. We were never going to battle "greed" through poverty or lack. As Jay W. Richards observes in *Money, Greed, and God*, although the Bible contains over 2,000 verses related to money and possessions, not one of them teaches that poverty is inherently virtuous or that wealth is inherently evil.[2]

Research in religious sociology reveals that early religious messaging about money can create cognitive patterns that persist for decades, influencing everything from a person's career choices, to their generosity and charitable giving.

As we prepare to tackle the issue of poverty and wealth, we must understand that this investigation serves a greater purpose than financial improvement alone. I want you to experience abundance, but the core problem to be solved is bigger than that. This is about aligning our understanding with God's original design for prosperity and stewardship. The blueprint is neither greed nor poverty. Both are damaging extremes that will compromise our ability to live a good life.

THE COST OF POVERTY

In 2013, researchers Anandi Mani, Sendhil Mullainathan, Eldar Shafir, and Jiaying Zhao conducted a groundbreaking study of Indian sugarcane farmers that revealed the cognitive toll of financial instability.[3] They found that the farmers performed significantly worse on cognitive tests before the harvest, when finances were tight, compared to after the harvest, when they had more resources. This fluctuation in performance was equivalent to a 13-point drop in IQ, or the effect of losing an entire night's sleep.

Poverty imposes a cognitive load that saps attention and reduces mental bandwidth, impairing decision-making and problem-solving abilities. This impairment isn't merely academic. It fundamentally changes how people navigate life's complexity. Even in a first-world economy like the United States or Europe, you will find people falling into patterns of living paycheck to paycheck. The mental strain of that scarcity leaves little room for long-term planning or financial resilience.

A 2016 study by Eileen Y. Chou, Bidhan L. Parmar, and Adam D. Galinsky, published in *Psychological Science,* found that economic insecurity increases physical pain, lowers pain tolerance, and leads to greater use of over-the-counter painkillers. Their research suggests that financial strain activates the same neural pathways as physical pain.[4]

Poverty doesn't just affect the brain; it also affects the soul, shaping behavior and moral judgment. When people experience long-term financial scarcity, they are more likely to cheat, steal, and compromise their view of right and wrong to escape the torment of never having enough.

A widely cited longitudinal study from the early 1970s, known as the Stanford marshmallow experiment, explored delayed gratification among children from various economic backgrounds. It revealed a pattern that confirms biblical wisdom about generational inheritance. [5]

Children from stable financial environments demonstrated a greater capacity to delay gratification and wait longer to get more marshmallows, a trait associated with future success and ethical decision-making. Children who came from economically unstable environments were more likely to take the immediate award, a behavior now understood as part of a "scarcity mindset." The research doesn't assign a moral value to poverty or wealth per se. It simply shows that our early financial environments shape our capacity to exercise wisdom.

The generational implications are profound. Modern psychological research confirms what Scripture has long suggested, that what we refuse to deal with in our lives will become our children's burdens. The Hebrew word *nachalah* (נַחֲלָה) refers not only to inheritance but of legacy, or material and spiritual transmission across generations. Both modern research and the ancient wisdom of the Bible say the same thing. You can either resolve these patterns in your own life, or your children will carry those burdens into theirs.

RIGHTEOUS ABUNDANCE

We see validation of righteous abundance throughout Scripture, from Abraham's wealth to Solomon's prosperity. The Greek word euodoō (εὐοδόω) used in 3 John 1:2 explicitly links spiritual and material prosperity together in God's design, which encompasses health (body), wealth (abundance), and wholeness (spirituality).

When it comes to money, the danger is in the extremes. To reject financial provision and abundance out of fear reveals a form of idolatry not dissimilar from the false worship of money. One side worships money because they are afraid of poverty. The other side worships lack because they are afraid of abundance.

The Greek word for the "love of money" (*philargyria* or φιλαργυρία) implies a pathological relationship with wealth that corrupts the soul. The opposite is no less unhealthy, as it requires an assumption that God is indifferent to our material well-being. Both sides are traps. To combat them, we have to learn to be comfortable in the tension of being "in the middle."

Psychological Effect	Poverty	Greed
Chronic Stress	Constant worry about bills	Constant fear of losing wealth
Short-Term Thinking	Focus on immediate survival	Focus on short-term profits
Poor Decision-Making	Impulsivity (loans, gambling)	Risk-taking (fraud, corruption)
Ethical Corrosion	Theft, scams	Exploitation, manipulation
Mental Distress	Depression, anxiety	Paranoia, insecurity

BACK TO THE GARDEN

Modern research findings are not just interesting scientific footnotes. They are a confirmation of ancient wisdom. The disconnect between our inherited design for abundance and our current experience of scarcity is spiritual at its core.

The Garden of Eden was God's original economic model. When we look back at the Garden, we are not just examining a historical location or a symbolic story. We are looking at humanity's original blueprint. It is a documented *design* parameter that still holds the key to how we were meant to function.

The economic principles we struggle to implement today were seamlessly integrated into Adam's original role of stewardship. His ability to manage creation was not just an administrative skill, but an expression of spiritual authority rooted in perfect communion with God.

This spiritual foundation helps explain why even our most sophisticated economic systems today often feel fundamentally incomplete. Many of them attempt to reconstruct order from chaos, but without addressing the spiritual foundations that were fractured in the Fall from Eden.

In the language of capitalism, Adam was humanity's first chief executive officer, and he operated at a level of competence that modern management theory can no longer conceptualize. He wasn't just living in paradise but actively managing and expanding the production of the entire world.

The cognitive demands of his position included naming every living creature, overseeing the order and rhythm of creation, and managing the full scope of the earth's resources. Modern neuropsychology suggests that such comprehensive task management would require extraordinary neural capacity, far beyond what we currently associate with human executive function.

Interestingly, this massive responsibility came without the burden of hardship or exhaustion. Toil and struggle were not introduced until Genesis 3:17. Before that, Adam's governance flowed with effortless competency. Even more surprising was the level of fulfillment that must have accompanied Adam's performance.

Modern psychologists have noticed a profound link between self-esteem and self-efficacy. *The Six Pillars of Self-Esteem* author Nathaniel Branden defines self-efficacy as an individual's confidence in their ability to think, make decisions, and handle the basic challenges of life.[6] By this measure, Adam was not only extraordinarily effective, but he was happy. He did not struggle with insecurity nor wonder if he was "enough." His identity and purpose were perfectly aligned.

Compare Adam for a moment to today's business titans, like Elon Musk, Jeff Bezos, and the late Steve Jobs. These figures exemplify human innovation and executive function at the highest level, yet even they reflect only a shadow of humanity's original managerial capacity.

Adam wasn't managing a tech empire or a global supply chain, but stewarding the entire earth. His leadership extended over creation itself, unburdened by scarcity, competition, or dysfunction. Where modern executives rely on teams, data, and constant recalibration, Adam operated in perfect unity with God, drawing on a spiritual clarity and cognitive wholeness that far surpasses our current models of high performance.

Of course, Adam's governance was not perfect. His mistake cast humanity from Eden. The consequences of Adam's failure rippled through history, creating what modern economists might call "systemic risk." The vulnerability of our entire system points back to this singular point of failure.

Imagine a mistake so big that it took 5,000 years to get under control, and you will get a sense of the enormity of Adam's failure. The issue had nothing to do with his management abilities, a bad investment, or a poor naming convention. The mistake was made in his heart.

Today's financial instruments and economic systems can be viewed as attempts to impose order on the chaos that Adam created. Mankind has attempted to contain financial lack through production, to contain the loss of life through peace treaties and armistices, and to contain the slow decline of order through the guardrails of checks and balances. Yet none of it is working.

When Adam turned away from God, creation itself turned away from Adam and became unfruitful and unproductive. The once-perfect system began to drift instinctively towards disorder and chaos. You do not need a degree in economic thermodynamics to know that all financial markets will drift towards entropy. Just as a hot cup of coffee naturally cools and a tidy room eventually becomes messy, economic systems, if left to their own devices, naturally descend into disorder.

Since humanity fell from our original state of effective governance, we have been locked in a negative feedback loop, continuously fighting to reconstruct order from the mess. If you have ever felt like your life is spinning out of control, you have experienced the natural consequences of Adam's management.

Understanding this helps explain why sustainable wealth creation requires more than just technical knowledge. It demands wisdom to create and navigate a fundamentally altered reality. You can change your circumstances, but first you just need to learn how and, more importantly, why.

ALTERNATIVE USE

A deeper analysis of modern economics reveals just how far our attempts at correction have drifted from the biblical model of stewardship and prosperity. Take, for example, communism, which represents perhaps the starkest deviation. The system envisions a classless, state-controlled economy where individual stewardship is replaced by collective ownership. There is no reward or consequence for how you *use* your money, only for whether you follow the approved system.

Biblical scholars note this system of governance runs counter to the individual accountability emphasized through the Bible. A clear example appears in the Parable of the Talents in Matthew 25:14–30, where three individuals are given varying sums of money, which they are required to eventually pay back.

The first two individuals invest the money, while the third buries and saves it. When the master returns, he blesses the first two and gives them even more. However, he curses the third man, the saver, and calls him wicked.

All three men made use of debt. They were given money with the expectation of repaying it. Scripture often warns against debt, emphasizing the dangers of becoming a borrower rather than a lender. Yet here, in a story told by Jesus Himself, debt serves as a tool for multiplication. If the purpose of debt is to multiply it, then it carries different connotations.

What I find interesting is the motive of the third individual who buried the money and did nothing. The Bible doesn't say that he saved the money because he didn't know what to do with it. It says that he saved it because he was afraid. Matthew 25:24–25 reads, "So I was afraid and went off and hid your talent in the ground. Look, you have what is yours."

This is a point we will return to later in the book, but it is important to note the lesson that fear is a danger to your financial future. Audit the motives of your heart. Whether you have the desire to be wealthy or not, fear will poison you.

Each individual carries a personal responsibility for his or her future. God is interested in helping you, but rarely will He move on your behalf if you refuse to accept responsibility for anything. Communism cuts off the accountability and responsibility of the individual and uses fear as an instrument of governance.

Socialism, while perhaps noble in its intentions, violates the biblical principle of reward for diligence (Prov. 12:24). In socialism, the state regulates major industries, and producers are penalized for being productive through taxes, regulation, and redistribution. This creates a condition where individuals stop trying to improve their circumstances, or "learned helplessness," which is antithetical to God's design for humanity.

Fascism, with its rigid social hierarchies, uniquely highlights humanity's failed attempt to recreate order through "top-down" control. This system directly contradicts the biblical principle of non-partiality (Acts 10:34) by replacing divine order with human authority structures. Under fascism, private businesses and property are allowed if they serve the state, and classism is installed to protect those at the top.

Central to understanding these deviations is the economic principle of "alternative use," which is the idea that resources are limited and must therefore be allocated to their most productive or meaningful use among competing options. This closely mirrors the biblical command for stewardship: to take what you are given, however small, and use it wisely, creatively, and with accountability.

Between 1990 and 2004, the number of Chinese citizens living in extreme poverty decreased from 374 million to 128 million through the implementation of alternative use principles.[7] However, the Communist state's failure to fully embrace economic agency has created what economists call a "sustainability paradox," which refers to short-term gains without long-term viability.

Research in developmental economics confirms that sustainable economic growth requires more than top-down policy changes. It requires individual participation in the economic process.[8] Since communism limits individual economic agency, China cannot instill alternative use principles into the population. They are locked in a back-and-forth battle that they will never fully win.

Stewardship is about personal adherence to the pursuit of wisdom. Your governor cannot do it for you. Your President cannot do it for you. You alone are responsible for your choices.

Contrast the outcome of China against India's economic transformation over the last few decades. The country's shift from socialist control to market-driven economics in 1991 led to a dramatic increase in GDP and per capita income, from $375 in 1999 to $1,700 by the mid-2010s.[9] This exemplifies what happens when a system aligns more closely with principles of individual stewardship and responsible resource management.

The simple but profound truth is that economic systems that move further from biblical principles of individual stewardship, responsibility, and creative resource management inevitably face challenges. However, this is a spectrum, not a dichotomy. The closer a civilization adheres to Biblical instruction, the better it will do. Neither the capitalistic system of America nor the communist system of China will fix this.

BIBLICAL FINANCIAL GOVERNANCE

The Bible provides profound insights into divine economic principles that transcend any specific historical context. These ancient accounts reveal sophisticated financial structures that mirror, and often surpass, modern economic theory.

God's monetary system was a covenantal theocracy. The rules decentralized everything and tied prosperity and increase to justice, caring for the poor, inheritance, and rest. Provisions would fall from the sky, or other people would just give their wealth to people destined to have it. It was a simple yet nuanced model that penalized greed and rewarded rest.

The Bible's financial rules were not random or ritualistic. They were a deliberate system designed to promote fairness, responsibility, and care within the community. Prosperity was connected to moral behavior, such as helping the poor and respecting family inheritance, ensuring society functioned with justice and sustainability.

Important legal structures surrounded land and business ownership. Generosity was condoned, but free handouts were warned against. Consider David's refusal to receive the gifted land in 2 Samuel 24. A man owned a plot of land, and David asked to buy it from him in order to build an altar there. This citizen of Israel offered to give the land to King David, but the King refused. He was unwilling to accept a handout when he had the means to purchase it from the man. This gives us a glimpse into God's system.

God repeatedly says that David was a man after God's own heart, which means we can see in David a mirror of the heart of God. How David thought and made decisions reflects how God makes decisions to a small but visible degree. God doesn't want to smother you with handouts. He wants you to partner with Him. Abundance is a partnership deal, not a one-way street of receiving.

Economists have studied and published a lot of research on what we call "stewardship deficiency." God understood it then, even if David didn't. Stewardship deficiency explains the consequences of unearned acquisition, resulting in a person's inability to manage well.[10] If you do not learn how to work the field, you will not be entitled to the food *from* the field.

JOSEPH, PRIME MINISTER OF EGYPT

The story of Joseph, found in Genesis 41, presents perhaps the most sophisticated economic case study in ancient literature. Joseph was sold into slavery and sent to Egypt. While in prison, Joseph discovered he could interpret dreams. Brought before the Pharaoh of Egypt, Joseph accurately predicted Egypt would experience seven years of abundance followed by seven years of famine. He advised that the Pharaoh store the surplus grain during the good years in preparation of the famine.

Joseph's divinely inspired resource management strategy wasn't just crisis prevention, but a masterclass in pricing, scarcity management, and resource allocation. Contemporary market theorists note that Joseph's model demonstrated perfect application of supply-demand equilibrium theory thousands of years before it was invented.

At the heart of Joseph's success was his ability to create real value, not just extract profit. He built a system that sustained millions of people during a regional famine, while also generating revenue for Egypt when neighboring nations came to buy grain. Recent empirical research supports this model. Companies that prioritize long-term value creation tend to outperform those focused solely on short-term profit extraction. Joseph's operation wasn't just morally grounded, but economically superior.

Biblical principles underpin much of modern business theory, though few recognize the origins. Joseph was also extraordinary at pricing the value he created, which reflects what modern economists might call a "dynamic pricing model."

To understand how dynamic pricing works today, think about the difference between a Ferrari and a Toyota. The price of a Ferrari is very different from the price of a Toyota. But why? A combination of supply-demand equilibrium and dynamic pricing.

Ferrari has only made 220,000 vehicles over 72 years (1947-2019). Toyota sells 10 million vehicles a year. That massive difference in supply affects the perceived value. The fewer there are of something desirable, the more people are willing to pay. Joseph did not sell the grain during the years of abundance when supply was high. He stored it and then priced the grain higher during years of scarcity when there was more demand.

Economic research shows that pricing typically reflects two fundamental indicators:

1. Resource availability (rarity)

2. Utility (efficacy)

The first part is that there are simply fewer Ferraris than Toyotas. The second function, utility, is less straightforward. A Ferrari's perceived utility is higher than a Toyota's. Notice that I said perceived utility. This is because the value of utility (what something does for you) is always changing.

I have owned exotic sports cars in my life, and they took me to the same places as the more affordable cars. If the utility were simply "transportation," there would be no sizable price difference. However, utility is a perception. When I drive a Porsche 911, I have more fun than when I drive a Chevrolet Silverado. Enjoyment is a form of utility or efficacy. Status is also a primal motivator for the human species, and I'd be lying if I said there wasn't a little bit of status involved in the purchase.

Rarity and efficacy also drive pricing for larger assets like real estate. A property's value is often correlated to its rarity. My house sits on five acres in a suburb of Nashville, Tennessee. If you were to build the exact same structure on the last available beachfront lot in Florida, the costs of the materials may not change much, but the value of the property would explode. Why?

As rarity increases, so does the price. If I'm on the last beachfront property available in Florida, the property is extremely rare. Economists have long recognized that location-based scarcity premium plays a critical role in property valuation. Industry estimates suggest that such premiums can range from 300 to 1,000 percent, depending on the rarity of the location and market conditions.

A 2023 study published in *Real Estate Economics* also found that property values near greened vacant lots increased by up to 19 percent in neighborhoods with a high share of vacant land (Lin, Jensen, and Wachter 2023).[11] Here, amenity scarcity functions as a micro-level example of the broader scarcity premium that defines high-value locations like beachfront property.

This principle isn't new. In fact, we see it at work thousands of years ago in Genesis 47 when Joseph begins executing one of the most forward-thinking economic systems in the Bible. The land of Egypt had gone into famine, and the crops and livestock were no longer sufficient for the population. Joseph was not taken off guard. He had been given divine insight and had stockpiled grain during the seven years of abundance.

The first lesson here is that divine insight often comes with divine strategy. If you ask God for something, He can give you future-oriented principles that may not make sense to anyone else but are exactly what is needed for what is to come. Joseph did not broadcast his strategy or warn anybody else. He secured the backing of the Pharaoh of Egypt to allocate resources before the famine hit. Not everything revealed to you is meant to be published on social media or shouted from the rooftops. There are times when God will give you wisdom and expect you to implement it quietly, with discipline and faith, long before others understand its value.

In the first year of the famine, people approached Joseph to buy food. The fair market value was likely high given that there was no food in Egypt, which means it was expensive. For a dynasty the size of Egypt, the amount of money spent on food would have been in the hundreds of millions, and potentially even billions, of dollars in today's terms.

In the second year, the people came back for more, but they were out of money. Instead, they offered their livestock in exchange. This effectively transferred all of Egypt's future food production and transportation to Joseph. The value of this livestock would have ordinarily been greater than the value of the stored grain. This represents a significant price increase for the food, yet people were willing to pay the higher price. Why? Because in the second year, there was even less grain than in the first year. As rarity goes up, so does the price.

In the third year, everyone came back again. They said, "We have no money and no livestock." Instead, they offered Joseph their land. Joseph accepted and instituted a permanent 20 percent tax on all future harvests. Once again, the price of grain had increased, and the people suggested it, not Joseph. In three years, Joseph now possessed all of the livestock, all of the money, and 5-7 million acres of land for Pharaoh without even breaking a sweat.

The most impressive asset in this story isn't the grain, the storehouses, or the economic pricing systems, but the intellectual and creative capital of the person who managed it. Joseph developed the ability to hear God and do what God instructed. When it comes to creating and stewarding wealth, this is the most important piece of it: As a result of heeding God's wisdom, Joseph made himself irreplaceable to the Pharaoh.

Over the years, I've had many staff. Some of them have been outstanding, but few of them have become irreplaceable. These are the individuals who end up managing entire companies or critical processes without needing my constant input. In modern management theory, Joseph would be classified as "irreplaceable executive talent."[12] When you have these people around you, it can drive outcomes and generate returns that exceed the status quo by orders of magnitude.

The Bible says that Pharaoh gave Joseph his signet ring, transferring executive and legal authority over the world's wealthiest nation (Gen. 41:42). The transfer of control over Egypt's labor, livestock, and capital assets wasn't merely delegation. It was the ancient world's most significant application of alternative use.

Imagine giving your chief operating officer unlimited authority by signing over your estate, money, house, and everything your family owns, and trusting them to run it. That's effectively what Pharaoh did when he promoted Joseph. It was an expensive decision for the Pharaoh, and yet he got the better end of the deal. It would have been far more costly not to promote Joseph than it was to give him everything.

When we align ourselves with the wisdom of God, we become timeless assets that can create exponential returns not only for ourselves but for others. But first, we must access *chochmat olam* חָכְמַת עוֹלָם)), the wisdom of the ages that only comes from God.

GOD WANTS TO FIGHT FOR YOU

"The LORD will fight for you while you [only need to] keep silent and remain calm."
—Exodus 14:14 (AMP)

Part of my job as a business consultant involves training business leaders on how to grow effectively. To do this, I have to travel frequently. On one routine trip to Orlando, I was scheduled to speak to more than 500 high-net-worth business owners. For me, it was just another day at the office, but sometimes God uses mundane things to change our lives forever.

It was hard at first to tell that anything was wrong. Traveling can be exhausting for someone with my personality. I'm always a bit on edge after being stuck on a plane with other people, and I often need to unwind as soon as I step off. Over time, I have refined a routine to help me maintain peak performance despite the drain of constant stimuli.

Twenty-four hours before the trip, I received a detailed document from my team mapping local gyms, restaurants, and important appointment times. Bottled water and snacks were delivered to my hotel so I could eat something and head straight to the gym. Unfortunately, this time, my routine was not working.

Neuroscience shows that physical exertion can reset everything from blood pressure to circadian rhythms. However, efficiency cannot address spiritual exhaustion. This trip to Orlando felt different because I stood at a crossroads with God, and exercise cannot remedy that.

I was preparing to travel to a bunch of business owners to teach them how to be successful, but I didn't feel successful myself. In retrospect, I was experiencing purpose fatigue. My external success had amplified my internal questioning rather than resolved it.

The human spirit can only sustain so much tension. When God's plans and your own are not lining up, even the strongest of wills begin to tire. The more stubborn you are, the longer it can take. I had finally hit a point where I was forced to be honest with God, not as a random, disinterested deity but as a father figure. For the first time, I started telling Him how I felt.

Looking back, I call this my "season of the drain." No matter how much money came in, the bills matched the income. One month, I'd set a new record for company revenue. The next month, we would break a record for how many things could fall apart and need to be fixed. Sometimes, when people hear me talk about money in a video or at an event, it will open the door to comparison. I will share something honest about the pressures I am feeling, and inevitably, someone in the crowd will say, "Well, at least you have money."

From the outside, it can be hard to imagine that financial stress exists on the other side of success. However, stress does not disappear with more zeros. It comes down to simple math. I would rather make $8,000 after spending $5,000 than make $1,000,000 but spend $1,200,000. In the season of the drain, it was a million dollars in, a million dollars out.

In the middle of this draining financial cycle, I was also wrestling spiritually. I had been asking God to help me out, but consistently heard nothing back. After a year of pleading for a sign, I told God that if He wanted me to keep doing what I was doing, He would need to give me confirmation. Like Moses, when he said in Exodus 33:15 (NIV), "If your presence doesn't go with us, I will not go."

What my heart deeply craved was rest. I dreamed of selling most of our things and retiring to a small house in a quieter city. Many people crave the big stages and bigger life, but I had already lived all of that, and it was exhausting. I just wanted to live on a farm and spend time with my family.

From the outside, I looked successful, and by many worldly standards, I was. Yet inside, my life felt like one meandering scenic route to nowhere. For years, I had rushed and sprinted and danced through the motions to build an empire. Once I had the empire, I didn't want it anymore.

The Bible says that people perish when they have no vision. I was perishing, not because I lacked resources, but because I was spinning in circles. Progress felt like a loop. It was one step forward and several steps back, over and over.

It isn't always poverty that kills you. Sometimes, the real thief is hope deferred. It is the quiet weight of mediocrity whispering that you should be doing more, earning more, or living more than you are now.

While most of us say we want to see God perform miracles, many of us avoid all situations that would allow God to produce a miracle in our lives. When you are fatigued, frustrated, confused, and at the end of your rope, that is when God acts.

In the middle of all that soul-weariness, I broke one of my die-hard rules. Typically, I limit myself to one project per trip. I live in Nashville, so it's easy to get in and out of most places. I never go from one city to another without first returning home to Nashville. This is how I make sure I get to see my family and don't end up on long, multi-week sprints away from home.

While I was duking it out with God, a friend called me to ask me a personal favor. There was a worship conference an hour away from Orlando, and he wanted to know if I would play music for it. I said no almost immediately. I still play at my home church a few times a month, but the days of touring around leading worship were long behind me. He asked me to think about it. As soon as he did, the Holy Spirit spoke and clearly told me to change my answer to yes.

I was extremely upset. Imagine sitting down with a friend for dinner and asking them a question. Instead of answering it, that friend starts answering a totally different, random, and unrelated question that you didn't ask them.

I thought to myself, *Really? You won't tell me what to do with my life, but you will drag me out to some random worship conference?*

Some people see me on videos talking about my relationship with God and think that I am being sacrilegious. They think that you should be more careful when you are talking to the architect of the universe, the King of Kings, the Lord of Lords.

While He is all of those things, He is also Father. In my experience, God has never had any issues with me arguing through something that I do not understand. He knows that I will eventually obey, but that sometimes I just need to talk it out. As He says in Isaiah 1:18 (NIV), "Come now, let us reason together" (Isa. 1:18). The more honest you are with Him, the more He will engage with you.

There's a parable Jesus tells in Matthew 21:28–31 (New Living Translation) about a man with two sons. He asked the older boy to go and work in the vineyard. The boy refused at first, but later changed his mind and went. The father then asked his younger son. This boy promised that he would, but he never did. Jesus then asked which son truly obeyed the father. The answer was the one who followed through, even if he initially said no. This story validates the struggle of wrestling honestly with faith. Our initial reactions do not define us; our ultimate actions do.

Writing a book about these concepts does not mean I have figured them all out. The gap between knowing and doing remains my battlefield. Psychologists call this the "knowing-doing gap," referring to the human tendency to understand something while failing to actually implement what we learn. Luckily, God makes space for our shortcomings.

My obedience is not predicated on whether it "makes sense" to me. However, I have a relationship with God that allows me to be obedient and still frustrated if I do not understand it. My prayers are not always "reverent" and composed: they can be messy. This is part of processing, and you have permission to wrestle with it. You would be surprised to know how often speaking my thoughts aloud helps to align my heart with something my head is resisting.

GIVING GOD AN INSTRUMENT

One of my mentors, Dale Mast, offered me a framework that transformed my approach to understanding God's instruction. "When you're trying to get an answer," he told me, "give God some notes to play. Then watch what He plays. Follow the music as He shows you through the notes."

This is a form of what psychologists call "hypothesis testing," where we create mental models of possible outcomes and then observe reality to confirm or reject our hypothesis. This way, we get to participate in the discovery process rather than passively waiting for clarity.[1]

One of the clearest biblical illustrations of this pattern is in the story of Gideon from *Judges* 6. Gideon is a man crippled by insecurity, who asked God for evidence of His existence before he was willing to take any action. While many made fun of Gideon for his lack of faith, God never did. He understands the human condition and works to help us move forward.

God appeared to Gideon and told him that he was to lead Israel in a liberation campaign against the Midianites. Gideon did not believe the message and essentially said, "I'm going to put this towel on the ground. Tomorrow, if the ground around it is dry, but the towel is wet, then I will believe you and obey." He gave God some notes to play and waited to see if God played them. The next morning, the towel was soaked, while the ground remained dry.

However, cognitive biases run deep. A single data point wasn't enough to overcome Gideon's limited mindset. He reversed the parameters, now asking for a dry fleece and wet ground. Again, God delivered without reprimanding him.

His divine patience aside, God understood Gideon's deeply personal, if silly, need for confirmation and chose to meet him there. If God can be that gentle with someone paralyzed by doubt, He's not going to get mad at you for wanting to talk it out.

Personally, I don't just want to hear about God. I want to experience God. To do this, you have to be honest with God and talk it out with Him.

I decided to do the same thing Gideon did and gave God three impossible things that were never going to happen and three very probable occurrences that would almost certainly happen by default. If the impossible things came to pass, I would take it as confirmation that I was on the right trajectory and trust that God was taking care of me. If the more likely things came to pass, I would stop what I was doing, downsize, retire, and disappear.

In the interim, I agreed to play at the conference. In my mind, I was going to wait for my out, and then I would do it my way.

AN ENCOUNTER WITH GOD

I was still very upset when I boarded my plane to the conference. Little did I know that He was preparing me for an encounter that I desperately needed. He was just doing it in a way that I could not control, and therefore did not trust.

God will open doors for you when He can trust you, but first, you must trust God enough to be honest with Him. In psychotherapy, studies show that genuine expression, especially when uncomfortable, accelerates progress more than polite compliance or surface-level politeness.[2] My willingness to be honest with God, even when it was messy, began to open up neural pathways that had long been closed due to my need for control.

The business conference was amazing. Thinking about it now, I can see a demarcation line between who I was before and after the event. I had stepped into a new anointing, though I did not know it then.

When you are obedient before you fully understand, you begin to operate at a different level in the spirit. The more desperate you are for God to talk to you, the more likely it is He will talk to you. These are basic principles that we will get into later in the book.

If you are a speaker, communicator, or author, there is a specific kind of anointing you can ask for that allows you to grasp God's heart for people in a way that goes beyond your natural skill and instinct. One of my desires for the church in America is for pastors to chase the anointing of God as much as they chase excellence.

There is nothing wrong with being excellent. In Exodus, God chooses a man named Bezalel to build the Tabernacle.

> *"I have filled him with the Spirit of God, giving him great wisdom, ability, and expertise in all kinds of crafts. He is a master craftsman, an expert in working with gold, silver, and bronze. He is skilled in engraving and mounting gemstones and in carving wood. He is a master at every craft."*
> —Exodus 31:2–5 (NLT)

Skill is important to God. He chose Daniel, the Jewish prophet who served in Babylonian politics, to influence kings and interpret His divine mysteries. The Bible says that Daniel was "ten times better" than all the magicians and enchanters in the kingdom (Dan. 1:20). The apostle Paul, too, was highly educated and well-trained as an orator, writer, and intellectual. In psychology, the concept of *earned authority* describes credibility that comes from demonstrated competence.

Excellence is desirable because it shows that you have the skills necessary to steward your assignment. However, it should never compete with anointing. If I show up with a lot of skill, it may be entertaining, but without anointing, it will never move people the right way or in the right direction. Neuroscience at least partially explains why. Research shows that technical information mainly engages the brain's analytical centers. Truly transformative communication reaches both the thinking and feeling parts of the brain at the same time.[3]

I am often invited to speak at events, and it has become an interesting game that I play with the Holy Spirit. You can tell when anointing begins to shift things around. At one point, it is no longer me doing the job I was paid to do, but the anointing speaking through me.

Anointing pierces the human heart just as knowledge pierces the human mind, but it operates on an entirely different dimension. I will often ask, before I speak or teach, "God, help me say what You want to say today." Later, when I am breaking down how it went, I will try to figure out when it shifted from me talking from my notes, to me flowing wherever the river wanted to go.

After the business event in Orlando, I woke up early and ordered an Uber to get my gear to the venue for the worship conference. I was tired, ready to get back home, which I had already put on the market to sell. I had not even waited for God to "play the notes." I assumed that He would stay silent, as he had all the previous year. I was ready to downsize, and I wasn't holding my breath for God to do any signs just yet.

THE INSTRUCTION OF GOD

In the Uber, I received an email from our realtor saying they had another showing. These potential buyers wanted to take a second look before they made an offer. As I was reading the note, my Uber driver asked me to take my headphones off. I did, and he said, "God wants me to share this story with you."

I was immediately intrigued. The driver said, "A few years ago, God asked us to move to Tampa from Alabama. God told me that He was going to provide a house on the beach for us to live in, and we would not have to pay for it."

A few weeks passed, and the man and his wife started praying that God would hurry up because they were putting their lives on hold to be obedient. Not long after, the phone rang, and sure enough, someone had a house on the beach they wanted to give to this man and his wife.

If I'm being totally honest, my initial response was resentful. I thought, *Sounds great. Good for you. God answers everyone except me.*

"There was only one problem with the house," the driver continued. "Want to know what it was?"

"Sure," I replied, still not understanding why he was even talking to me.

He replied, "The house wasn't in Tampa. And God told us to go to Tampa."

Now I was invested in the story. "See? It's never that easy, is it? So what did you do? Did you give God an ultimatum?"

The man told me that he and his wife prayed about it again and felt that God had been very specific, so they waited. A few weeks later, just as they were about to move on, another call came. This time, the person had a house on the beach in Tampa and offered it to them.

"Wow, that is a crazy story," I said as I moved to put my headphones back on. I was almost discouraged that it had worked out for this man. I knew intuitively that this was the wrong thing to feel. You can sometimes tell by your instinctive feelings how far you've drifted from how God wants you to live. I knew that I should not be upset that God had helped this man, but my instincts had been programmed by years of hope deferred.

That was when the man said, "Taylor, when God gives you a promise, the enemy will always give you something that looks just like the promise, but it is not 100 percent of the promise. You have to decide whether you are going to last until the promise comes, or if you will take the counterfeit option. You must use your faith to reject the counterfeit, even if it seems good. If it is not fully God, it will not protect you the way you think it will."

I recognized this as the first of several "God moments" that I would experience over the next few days. God can speak to you through a podcast, a book, or a random Uber driver in Tampa. Like all messages from God, this one pushed me into deep reflection.

How many times in our lives have we been certain that God is setting something up for us? Then, in the process of waiting, we find a way to cut corners or "tweak" the situation, as if we would do God a favor by making His job easier. Every time I have done this, I have looked back and realized I made things worse instead of better.

This idea is supported by psychological research, particularly in a concept known as the "amygdala hijack," a widely recognized term coined by psychologist Daniel Goleman in his book *Emotional Intelligence* (1995).[4] Fear primes the body for survival, not strategy. When we are afraid, we often make it worse by responding disproportionately.

We also see this principle illustrated in Scripture. King Saul, who was afraid of losing power, acted in the interest of keeping his power. Ironically, it was this behavior that ultimately caused him to lose power. In 1 Samuel 15:24, King Saul admits, "I have sinned... because I feared the people and obeyed their voice" (ESV).

Our job is not to do favors for God, but to obey and to trust that, in our obedience, God will take care of us. Sitting in the Uber on the way to the venue, I realized for the first time that God did not need me to protect myself. His silence had not meant He had nothing to say. He was waiting for me to stop trying to speak and act on His behalf. In the quiet, he was saying, "I will defend you when you get tired of defending yourself."

The waiting was instructive, not punitive. It also did not have to do with whether I sold everything, quit working, and played small, or kept going. It wasn't about my lifestyle at all. The real issue was my attempt to reconcile what God had promised me with the lack I perceived in between. The middle is always messy because that is when we try to become God for ourselves and force His promises to happen through our skills or intellect.

When I arrived at the venue, I checked my phone before unloading. To my surprise, one of my impossible items I had asked God to perform as a "fleece test" had been checked off the list. By the time I got to the airport the next day, the other two had also been fulfilled.

His message to me felt clear: "Do not back down. Do not play small. I've got this, but you are causing chaos in the middle. First, deal with your trust issues, and then we will advance."

This is how God has always worked throughout history. My experience in Orlando was a small window into an eternal pattern. He meets us in our moments of crisis and confusion, not to shame us, but to reveal Himself and His ways more clearly.

What I experienced personally in that Uber ride, and earlier on stage at the conference, was actually part of a much larger story, and a divine narrative that stretched across time. To understand this fully, we need to pull back the curtain and look at God's character through a wider lens.

When we examine the grand tapestry of Scripture, we see that God has always been engaged on behalf of His people. The God of War is not simply a title. It is a revelation of His commitment to fight for what belongs to Him.

THE GOD OF WAR

"The LORD is a warrior. Yahweh is his name."
—Exodus 15:3 (NLT)

Orlando was a turning point where I stopped thinking of God as a responder and began seeing Him as a strategist. A warrior. Not reactive but orchestrating.

God is not disinterested. In fact, he is personally invested. When you realize God is not only good but intentional, your entire life changes. But to fully trust Him, we have to understand something of His nature. The more we learn about how He thinks, the bolder we become in how we live.

In 2007, cognitive psychologist Gary Klein introduced a concept that secular thinkers hailed as revolutionary, but which God's people have actually practiced for centuries. Known for his work studying decision-making under pressure, Klein called this tool the "premortem," similar to a postmortem but done in advance.

In his Harvard Business Review paper, "Performing a Project Premortem," Klein examined the idea of analyzing failure before it happens as a psychological tool to prevent failure. Klein's invention is predated by the Stoic practice of *premeditatio malorum*, or the premeditation of evils, in which individuals mentally rehearse potential misfortunes to build resilience. Roman emperor and Stoic philosopher Marcus Aurelius, writing in the second century A.D., also encouraged anticipating adversity as a form of mental preparedness.

Yet long before the Stoics, the Bible had already outlined this mode of strategic foresight. Scripture repeatedly encourages us to anticipate challenges, consider the cost, and seek wisdom before we act.

The capacity to anticipate, reflect, and plan is not random. It is embedded in how God designed us. We are made in the image of Yahweh, and thus have certain access to different psychological capacities that reflect how God thinks.

Strategic foresight isn't just a human trait, but a divine one. That is why when I read Scripture, I want to know what happened, why it happened, and what lessons I can extract from the story and apply to my life today.

To be exceptional, you must have the courage to imagine your problems and choose to move past them. In my work across many different industries and with people from all walks of life, I have observed that many people approach their circumstances through dangerous biases.

One is the belief that just being born makes you special. Another is believing that people deserve success simply because they work hard. Real, lasting success often requires more than effort or good intentions. It asks for a deeper kind of wisdom, one grounded in truth.

The truth is that humans were not meant to earn everything through striving alone. We are meant to partner in it. However, that will always come at a cost.

That's why it is important to think about what something costs before we pursue it. This principle is called *opportunity cost awareness*, or the ability to recognize that choosing one path means giving up another. Cost isn't just measured in dollars or time, but in focus, freedom, and other opportunities. Someone who understands opportunity cost awareness develops the discipline to delay gratification and do the right thing now without expecting immediate, short-term results.

Jesus referenced this in Luke 14:31: "Have you ever heard of a commander who goes out to war without first sitting down with strategic planning to determine the strength of his army to win the war against a stronger opponent?" This is essentially a premortem, or a warning, to think it through before you move.

He returns to this theme in Matthew 10:16 (NKJV): "Behold, I send you out as sheep in the midst of wolves. Therefore, be wise as serpents and harmless as doves." He is not just offering poetic imagery, but describing a kind of mental readiness. His language suggests a spiritual war game, or a structured exercise in which you are asked to imagine how a future scenario will unfold. Then, in that awareness, you can ask God for wisdom. This is a piece of psychological technology that you can deploy in any area of your life to make better decisions.

Before executing a strategic maneuver, military commanders typically run simulations to test scenarios and anticipate outcomes. This was another idea that came from God. David wrote in Psalm 82:1 (ESV), "God has taken his place in the divine council; in the midst of the gods, he holds judgment." God sat down with his rulers and guided them through a structured process. In his wisdom, he taught them how to impose order. In the end, they were judged for going against His way.

In this chapter, I want to take you through a story where we get to see how God thinks and operates. It is important to acknowledge that we will never be able to fully comprehend his divine mind, though we can glimpse facets. The human mind can only contain so much data and our consciousness is limited. As David confesses in Psalm 139:17 (ESV), *Ve-li mah-yaqaru re'ekha El, mah-atzmu roshéihem* ("How weighty are Your thoughts, O God? They are like gold, dense with glory and wonder," a cultural and more modern application).

One does not sit at the council of the Most High without being overwhelmed by the thoughts that proceed from the mind of El Elyon, the Most High God. However, we can connect the dots in retrospect and begin to find patterns in how God leads.

THE WAR OF THE AGES

We find ourselves, you and I, in the middle of a battle between two ancient and intelligent kingdoms. Long ago, the one true God participated in the war games of heaven. He assigned rulers, or lowercase *elohim*, to oversee different territories, which casts new light on the cost of Adam's fall. In the beginning, there was one ruler placed on earth to govern. When Adam was cast out of the council of heaven, many rulers were assigned to take his place.

Somewhere along the way, the authority assigned was misused. The *elohim* or "divine beings" became arrogant and corrupted. Ever since Adam's fall, humanity has lived in the shadow of that rebellion. There was mutiny before the creation of man, and there was mutiny after. The crooked serpent, the dragon, seeded his whispers everywhere across creation.

For the second time, the Most High God personally intervened to restore order in a kingdom reeling from chaos and betrayal. Lest you be confused about the nature of the true God, He is a God of war. While he is a God of restoration, too, against His enemies, it is war.

He is vehemently protective and worthy of trusting. Nahum 1:2 says, *"Nāqōm wĕ-nōtēr YHWH, nōtēr YHWH ū-baʿal ḥēmāh; nōtēr YHWH lĕ-tzarāv, wĕ-nōtēr hūʾ lĕ-ʾoyĕvāv."* The retranslation of this Hebrew statement shows us a picture of YHWH: "Yahweh is a fiercely protective God, zealous with covenantal fire. He executes divine justice upon oppressors and preserves wrath for those who persist in enmity against Him."

God's wrath is targeted. It is not a generalized rage but a holy response to His people's oppression. We find many great examples of this throughout the Bible. One of my favorites is the story of Exodus. Contrary to how they are presented in the American Sunday school classes, the miracles God inflicted upon the empire of Egypt are not random.

OVERTHROWING AN EMPIRE

In 1991, Michael Jordan's Chicago Bulls were playing the Denver Nuggets, and Jordan was in the zone. He started trash-talking Dikembe Mutombo, an eight-time NBA All-Star and one of the best defensive players of his time. Jordan told Mutombo he would shoot both free throws with his eyes closed to prove he did not need his vision to make the shot.

Eyes closed. Shoots. *Swish.*

When you trash-talked Jordan, he played even better. He

could silence anyone by running them ragged all over the court and scoring on them at the same time.

A few years later, during a different game, one of Jordan's teammates, Dennis Rodman, was caught standing at half-court while Jordan was shooting free throws. Players are expected to be down by the shooter to get a rebound if the shooter misses. One of Rodman's teammates tried to get Rodman to move down the line. Rodman simply shrugged and ignored him. A reporter later asks Rodman what he was doing. Rodman replied, "Why would I get down there and rebound? It's not like he ever missed."

This is how the Old Testament reads. God is proving a point in everything He does. He doesn't miss, and He wants the *elohim* and the powers of the earth to know that He is the best player on the field.

Most Christians are monotheists, believing in one God: Yahweh. While it is true that there is one *supreme* God, it is not accurate to say there are no other gods. Why would one of the Ten Commandments instruct the Israelites to have "no other gods before me" if that were the case?

The *Most High* God, Yahweh, granted dominion to other beings meant to manage and govern for Him. These entities are significant and legitimate. Paul references them as principalities and rulers. There is a power structure in the kingdom of darkness that attempts to copy the kingdom of light.

Ancient civilizations organized themselves around their religions and their gods. The Canaanites worshipped their gods (lowercase). The Egyptians worshiped theirs, as did the Babylonians. God, El Elyon, was engaged in strategic warfare against these gods. When he showed up and began to defend and prepare His people, He targeted the gods of these other civilizations.

It began when he chose a tribe of people, the Israelites, and began to display his power. He chose an obscure, unknown man living in a pagan society named Abram. As Joshua 24:2 (NLT) states, "Long ago your ancestors, including Terah, the father of Abraham and Nahor, lived beyond the Euphrates River, and they worshiped other gods."

This gives us a glimpse into God's personality. He is not looking for the obvious choice. In 1 Samuel 16:7 (NLT), we see it again: "The LORD doesn't see things the way you see them. People judge by outward appearance, but the LORD looks at the heart." God didn't find a powerful personality or a king to build his people around. He found Abram, who would one day be called Abraham.

Out of this man, he begins to build a people of his own to frustrate the power-hungry deities of the earth. By the time we get to the story of Exodus, some six hundred years after God selects Abraham, his people are slaves in Egypt.

Yahweh steps in to reset the playing field, but this time, He makes it personal. Instead of a random person, His plan this time is to plant someone in enemy territory and use them to undo the entire system of government from the inside.

Moses, *or Moshe* in Hebrew, was raised in the courts of Egypt. There are nuances in the story of Moses that are often overlooked in how he is portrayed in the Sunday school version of the story. When I read the accounts, both biblical and historical, I can see the infinite complexities of how God moves through history.

Moses was adopted by none other than the Pharaoh's daughter. The historian Josephus called her Thermuthis, but we do not really know what her name was. All we know is that a Hebrew baby was taken and adopted in secret, then groomed to be in a position of power. Acts 7:22 (NIV) says that "Moses was educated in all the wisdom of the Egyptians and was powerful in speech and action." He wasn't simply going through school in Egypt but being trained for something important. Some scholars believe that he was in line to be one of the subsequent powerful rulers of Egypt.

We will never know until we get to heaven, but it is plausible that the original plan for Moses could have been very different. Whatever the enemy can do, God can do it better. Everything that happens in this realm begins with the words of your mouth. The serpent corrupted Adam and Eve with a word. If Moses had become the Pharaoh of Egypt, he could have freed the Hebrew slaves with a word, and that would have been the end of it.

However, Moses saw an Egyptian beating up a Hebrew slave, and grew angry. He killed the Egyptian man, and the ruler of Egypt was livid. A high-ranking member of the Egyptian elite betrayed the empire. This was the same temper that later caused Moses to violate God's instruction and be blocked from entering the promised land with his people.

You can see the hand of the enemy at work here. If he can get you to lose yourself to your passions, he can maneuver you out of positions of power and into powerless situations. The plan must be agile.

God did not abandon Moses, nor did He give up on the outcome. Understand fully that God does not lose, though human missteps can delay things. Moses was an outcast in the desert for forty years, and in that period, the old king of Egypt died.

The deities in Egypt had successfully delayed the inevitable. All the enemy does is delay the inevitable. However, God's ultimate plan remains in play. He used Moses to restore order and set his people free.

It doesn't matter if you seek to free people from financial insignificance, relational torment, psychological issues, or health complications. If you are going to play for God, this will always be true: You are a weapon in God's hands, and you will bring freedom to those around you.

THE GODS OF EGYPT

Setting the Israelites free was not God's only goal. This was now about judgment. In Exodus 12:12 (AMP), it says, "Against all the gods of Egypt I will execute judgments [demonstrating their worthlessness]. I am the LORD." This was about much more than just reclaiming His people. It was a statement: "You mess with what is mine, and I will come after you. So play your games at your own risk."

The plagues He sends to Egypt are *taunts*. Like Elijah on the top of Mount Carmel when he confronted the prophets of Baal, God asked, "If your gods are truly all-powerful, why can't they take care of their own? Where are they now?" The plagues that assaulted the Egyptian empire were chosen specifically to target the gods worshipped by the Egyptian people, who used the gods as justification for their cruelty toward the Israelites.

When Yahweh turned the Nile River into blood, he challenged the Egyptian gods Hapi (the god of the Nile) and Osiris (whom the Egyptians believed had his blood flowing through the Nile River), who could do nothing but watch. When the frogs appeared and started polluting everything, it was a character assassination of the Egyptian goddess Heqet, who was the goddess of water and bore the head of a frog. Again, she could do nothing but watch.

Most of us do not grasp the significance of these stories when we learn them as children. The liberation of the Hebrew people from Egypt was a full-blown war of the gods, with one ruler at the top. El Elyon was reminding both the gods and the people who was in charge.

The Egyptians had another deity called Geb, the god of the earth. What does Yahweh do? He overwhelms the land with the power He gave to Geb and used it against the dynasty. God (Yahweh) commanded Aaron to strike the ground and stir up the dust, which spontaneously ignited into millions of gnats that swarmed through Egypt. That, too, was a taunt. It said, "Where is Geb now? This is your god? Why is Geb doing this to you? Can he not save you?"

There are many examples of this side of God in Scripture. The Egyptian god Hathor, depicted with a cow's head, was believed to oversee livestock and agriculture, which were crucial for feeding and supporting the empire. Then Yahweh spoke and every living animal in Egypt stopped breathing.

The sky goddess Nut, associated with Set, the god of storms, was overwhelmed by God's judgment when He caused hail to fall from the sky and unleashed a wave of storms that tore apart Egypt's infrastructure.

The story of Exodus had ten plagues, and with each one, Yahweh moved progressively up the hierarchy of gods. The oldest and most powerful deity in Egypt was Ra, the god of the sun. The Egyptians believed that Ra would depart every night to battle the forces of chaos. This is why the sun set each evening. When he returned victorious, the sun would rise again.[1]

All the gods share a common desire to be like the one true God, so they attempted to create structures and names that resembled Him. Ra called himself the "creator" and the "king of the gods," titles which are sacred. For the ninth plague, God told Moses, "Stretch out your hand toward the sky, so that darkness may cover the land of Egypt, a darkness so terrible that it can be felt" (Exodus 10:21 AMP).

An entire empire of people was consumed with fear. If you were an Egyptian worshipping Ra, the implications would have been grim. Ra, your creator god, had apparently been defeated. He would not return for three days, so he must have been trapped or dead. If your most powerful god was so easily subdued by this new God, Yahweh, the inevitable conclusion was that you would die at the hands of Him. The Bible says this darkness was supernatural and oppressive, so deep that it could be "felt."

The God of Israel waited three days to relinquish the darkness. Again, the act was nothing but a statement to the polytheistic pantheon of Egypt not to touch what was His.

After Ra, there was one remaining "god" in Egypt that had to be dealt with: the Pharaoh. The Egyptians believed the Pharaoh was a living deity on earth, Horus. When a Pharaoh died, he was replaced with a new body, which Horus inhabited.

The first nine plagues of Egypt targeted the gods of the empire, but the tenth and final plague changed the stakes. The first nine gods existed in the supernatural realm, but Horus existed in the physical plane. In the first nine plagues, Yahweh took the power of the intangible gods and turned it against the very jurisdictions that the gods promised to help. However, in the tenth plague, he erased the physicality of Egypt and Egypt's future.

After Ra, the Egyptian people would've likely believed that they had been defeated, but that they could rise again. Horus, after all, could have just inhabited a different body and rebuilt it to its previous stature. Yahweh, therefore, attacked the hereditary or dynastic succession of the empire. For the tenth and final plague, He took the next in line and eliminated the legacy of the current Pharaoh "god" from existence. The defeat was final.

GOD'S STRATEGIC WARFARE

Have you ever wondered why spiritual battles feel so intense? Why doesn't God just snap His fingers and make everything the way it should be? I have wrestled with this question for years, watching people fight through challenges that seemed unnecessary with a God that is all-powerful.

The answer lay in understanding two truths about God that seem in conflict with each other. First, God is all-powerful and can do anything at any time. He is sovereign. However, and this is important, God is thorough and systematic. He doesn't just fix problems to fix them. He transforms entire situations, addressing every layer that needs to be addressed.

Think about a skilled surgeon removing a tumor. Can't they just quickly cut it out? Sometimes. However, a great surgeon thinks about more than just the tumor. They are also thinking about how to prevent infections, protect nearby organs, and ensure the person can recover after it's removed. It takes more time, but the results are better. We see this in the story of the Israelites in Egypt. God was not just trying to get His people out of Egypt; He was tackling several big problems at once.

He had had enough of the false gods pretending they could rival Him. It was the equivalent of a champion (human) boxer eliminating his competitors one by one. Each plague was a title belt stripped away from an *elohim* who had been left unchecked for too long. As you see from Scripture, the plagues weren't random, but extremely targeted.

His second purpose was to send a message to other nations to think twice before getting in His way and attacking His people. After Moses led the people out, God caused the Pharaoh to change his mind and go after them. God hardened the Pharaoh's heart because he wanted to send a message. When the soldiers went after the Israelites, God drowned them all.

That, too, was about more than simply spite or protecting his people only in that moment. God knew that His people would need to walk into enemy territory after they left Egypt. The story of their victory would read like a giant, blinking warning for the nations that would one day challenge Israel.

Many years later, when Joshua was taking Jericho, Rahab (a person living in Jericho) said to a spy, "Everyone here is terrified of you." That was because the story of Egypt had spread. Everyone knew what had happened, and they did not want to be the next military body at the bottom of the sea.

His third and hardest purpose was teaching His people to trust Him again. Someone who has been stuck in an abusive relationship for years will need time to believe they can be free, even after they are safe. The Israelites had been slaves for several generations. God needed to show them they could trust him. His actions were essentially saying, "I took care of you. When everything was going wrong, I was trustworthy."

Still, the people of Israel did not heal quickly. A few short weeks after seeing all these miracles, they needed another reminder of God's faithfulness. This was not because they were stupid or ungrateful. Slavery had been their reality for so long that freedom felt unnatural.

Many prisoners struggle with life after freedom. Aleksandr Solzhenitsyn spent eight years in a Russian Gulag and remarked that many released inmates would quickly commit petty crimes just to get back to prison, where they felt safer. He writes, "A man accustomed to a cage finds freedom unbearable." This gives us not only a glimpse into the Israelites but also into our own lives.

The Israelites might have been removed from Egypt, but it would take many years for Egypt to be removed from their minds. They thought like slaves, made decisions like slaves, and doubted their destiny as slaves do.

This is why our spiritual battles feel longer than necessary. God is not just changing our circumstances. He is changing how we think, how we see ourselves, and what we believe about Him. He is not just delivering us, but transforming us. God's strategy was perfect. His timeframe simply exceeded what the Hebrews had anticipated.

Sometimes we think that God is not moving quickly enough. Most of the delays we encounter have nothing to do with God but our own learning curves. Like Moses losing his temper, or the Israelites doubting God at the Promised Land.

What do we expect God to do? If He moves too quickly, we may ruin it in our attempt to possess the Promised Land without the means to keep it. If He moves too slowly, we express our displeasure, not realizing the timing issues are about *us*, not Him.

Modern Christians often poke fun at the Israelites. "How could they be so foolish? How could they lose faith in God so quickly?" The issue is not that they forgot about God. It's that they couldn't forget their identity as slaves.

Contemporary research in behavioral economics and psychological conditioning reveals how deeply entrenched our poverty mindsets can become after major setbacks. I recognize this in my own life, which draws a psychological parallel to the Israelites' immersion in Egyptian slavery.

We must root out this "slave" mindset that tilts our hearts toward poverty. Unless we slow down and get to the true culprit, we will inevitably forfeit our right to exist in abundance. Physical liberation from Egypt will not translate to immediate flourishing in a new tax bracket.

The good news is that the Israelites eventually ended up being successful. The bad news is that within just a few generations, the people of God had stopped worshipping the Most High God altogether. In their attempt to escape slavery, they turned to worship something far worse, highlighting the risk of success removed from faith.

THE RISE OF BAAL

In Egypt, we witnessed the ruling pantheon of Ra, Osiris, and Heqet—*elohim* that demanded systemic order. The geographical transition to Canaan introduced not merely new territory, but an entirely different spiritual jurisdiction belonging to the Canaanite gods of Baal, Astarte, Dagon, and Molech. These new gods operated within familiar frameworks, but were sneakier.

The problem for the Israelites, and for us in the present, is something theologians call "transferable bondage." Transferrable bondage refers to something that will stick with you, even following you into new territory, unless you remove the bondage.

Principalities, rulers, and demonic entities exist inside a legal system. The theology of grace does not apply to them. They are stuck in an old operating system and do not receive access to the mercy of God.

God allows them to operate in this system until their final day of judgment. However, because of the legal system of dominion (which has been restored to us, through Jesus) and grace, they are not allowed to kill you. Their job is not always to destroy you. Sometimes their strategic role is convincing you to open yourself up to them. In doing so, you give them legal rights they would never have had. This creates transferable bondage you carry with you, whether it's to a new city where you move, or a generational transfer that opens them up to your children.

In the opening chapters of this book, I was wrestling with feeling abandoned by God. The feeling had less to do with where I had been and more with where I was going. The journey God allowed me to go on would end up clearing me of transferable bondage that would have followed me into my new territory.

If the enemy had been successful in getting me to agree with him about myself or God, he would've opened up legal access to step into my future. This is an ongoing process because I cannot see the future and don't know precisely where God is taking me. The enemy often has a better idea of where God is taking us than we do. I've had to repent many times for things I have said in moments of frustration, because a legal contract in the spirit is a *word,* and we are held captive by our words. When God created everything, He didn't sign His name on a dotted line. That was not necessary. He *spoke.*

THE WORD OF THE ENEMY

You'd be amazed at how many beliefs, emotions, and traumas are strategically planted for the purpose of getting us off track. The serpent has been around for a long time and has studied human nature extensively. If God calls you to something, the enemy will deploy tactics to confuse you, and childhood is the perfect time to start.

Not long ago, my daughter was playing Monopoly with a friend. She played well for a six-year-old, but began to lose her composure towards the end. When she ran out of Monopoly money, she burst into tears in front of everyone.

I understand. Nobody likes to lose. However, as her father, I recognized that these tears seemed deeper, more heartfelt, and indicated something more was going on. She kept saying, "I always lose my money. I always lose my money."

I asked the Lord for help as I picked her up to hold her. I told her she could cry while I carried her to the other room. An idea hit me on the way in, and I believe it was the Holy Spirit guiding my thinking.

I picked up my iPad and handed it to her. "Here," I said, "can you draw how you're feeling on this so we can talk about it?" One of the first things you learn in psychology is psychological diffusion, or the ability to separate yourself from how you feel, so you can observe it objectively.

Kids have to learn this skill. When they don't know how to practice diffusion, it creates the opposite effect: emotional fusion. They cannot tell the difference between a feeling and their identity. I wanted her to practice getting her feelings outside, on an iPad, so that we could discuss them.

After about ten minutes, she handed it back to me. I saw two kids with big, sad expressions drawn on their faces. In the middle was a box with what looked to be money. When I asked her to explain the drawing, she told me softly through her tears that the kid on the left was her when she lost her money in her piggy bank. The kid on the right was her when she lost her money in Monopoly. Then came the real issue: "Daddy, no matter what happens, I can't keep money. I just keep losing all my money."

In her mind, this was a pattern, first with the piggy bank money, and now with the Monopoly money. This wasn't about losing a game. It was about an emotion trying to fuse with her identity, and the words she kept saying ("I always lose my money") were creating an agreement.

The Holy Spirit is smarter than I am. It was the Holy Spirit who gave me the idea to have her draw it out in the first place. My psychology training kicked in, and in that moment, I understood that this was a strategy, deployed effectively by the enemy of our destinies, to get my six-year-old to hand over legal rights.

If she spoke the statement, "I always lose my money," and believed it, some principality would one day use it as a permission slip to make it true in real life. I picked her up again and said, "Kate, losing things feels bad, but we are going to pray that God will bring us more. And then we are going to try and trust Him and tell Him that we know He will bring us whatever we need."

She was six, so it would not have been appropriate to lecture her on the legal weight of her own words. Instead, we prayed. She repeated the words after me, and the issue was resolved. She said "Amen," and bounced out of the room like nothing had happened.

That moment with my daughter revealed something profound about the enemy's strategy, which is that your real issue will always be revealed in words. Every declaration is a transaction in the spirit realm. The enemy understands this legal principle better than most Christians do. When we grasp the true nature of words as spiritual legal tender, we begin to see why both God and the enemy are so interested in what comes out of our mouths.

WORDS CAN BRING LIFE OR DEATH

The Israelites faced every conceivable battle. If the Israelites were children in middle school, they were picked last in every sport. If you have ever felt dumb, insignificant, or unimportant, like when I started my first business and only got attention for being obnoxious or failing, that was the experience of the Israelites. They were promised a land flowing with milk and honey, yet spent decades wandering in the desert, often doubting the very God who rescued them from slavery.

Have you ever won big, only to mess it up because you did not know how to maintain your momentum? After my first "big month" in business eleven years ago, I took my wife out to celebrate at what we had considered a fancy restaurant, Red Lobster. The next month, I had one of the worst months ever. I had let myself get entitled and stopped doing what was working. That, too, was the Israelite story. After conquering Jericho in a miraculous way, they faced a small city called Ai and were utterly defeated because of one man's sin, highlighting how quickly they could lose what they had gained.

The Israelites were the weakest tribe, with the fewest resources, and constantly fighting in enemy territory, without the home-field advantage. They were a small band of former slaves up against powerful empires like Egypt, and later Assyria and Babylon. And yet, God kept showing up for them.

Somehow, they survived and advanced despite their foibles. After Egypt, they wasted years screwing around. God performed miracles, proving that He had their backs, by parting the Red Sea, providing food and water from rocks, and even guiding them with a pillar of cloud by day and fire by night. Yet as soon as the next challenge showed up, they rejected Him, not because of Him, but because of their own overwhelming fear.

This is evident in the famous account of Joshua and Caleb. The Israelites got up to the demarcation line of their next assignment, which was to take the Promised Land. In Egypt, they were slaves, and God had to do everything for them. Then God expected them to graduate from this early "parenthood" situation to a partnership. They did not really have to trust God in the Exodus from Egypt, but they had to partner with God to take over Canaan. That next phase required their active faith, courage, and obedience.

Twelve spies were sent to investigate the land God told them to take. Ten returned with horror stories, claiming that they would all die. Only two trusted God enough to move forward.

Moses pleaded with them to trust God, but the people revolted. When the promise looked difficult, they betrayed God. As recorded in Numbers 14:2–4, the entire nation wept and sinned with their words: "Oh that we had died in Egypt! Or in this wilderness! Why is the LORD bringing us to Canaan to die by the sword? Our wives and children will become plunder. Wouldn't it be better to return to Egypt?" They even said, "Let's appoint a new leader and go back to Egypt."

What happened next served as a terrifying warning. God took the Israelites at their word. He told Moses in Numbers 14:28–29, "Say this to them, 'As I live, just what you have spoken in My hearing I will certainly do to you; your dead bodies will fall in this wilderness, all who were counted from twenty years old and up, who have complained against Me.'"

The people did not like this response and changed their minds. However, they did not change their hearts or repent of their words, which we know to be spiritual legal contracts. The Israelites were motivated by punishment, not genuine trust. They modified their behavior without adjusting their trust levels.

God's promises do not just depend on us changing our conduct. If they did, we could earn our way in and out of His kingdom. His promises rest on the attitudes of our hearts. In this case, the Israelites gave us an expensive case study to learn from.

Moses, again, pleaded with them, but in reverse. He told them not to go forward out of fear of judgment. He essentially told them, "God has spoken. You have no business trying to change your minds before you talk to God."

Poor Moses was stuck in the middle. He urged the people to trust God by going forward, and then urged them to trust God by not going forward. I often hear preachers talk about the power of "God-sized" dreams, urging people to aim higher and dream bigger. I understand their intentions, and any genuine dream from God will likely be significant, but setting bigger goals is not how we get to God, nor does it guarantee His backing. Heaven's currency is trust, not ambition. Winning in God's kingdom requires big trust, not just big vision.

I recently had one of my honest moments with God. I love God more than anything else, but there are still areas in my heart where I struggle to trust Him. I have told Him this, and even if I had not, He would still know.

When I feel this way, I take a moment to quickly audit my words. I never want to invite the enemy's economy into my home by constantly complaining. It is okay to be frustrated, and it is okay to talk to God when you are frustrated. However, we must understand that the words we speak when we are upset will either enforce a promise or create a curse.

The Holy Spirit showed me things I have said recently that did not enforce God's promises, and therefore opened me up to the enemy's legal influence. I repented and renounced them. Rather than forcing ahead based on an old promise from God, I now seek God's backing to enforce His own words in my life.

I would encourage you to pause and repent for any words you have spoken in anger or frustration. Remind yourself that if God is for you, nothing else has a chance of standing against you. Speak it out loud and repeat this: "The goodness of God will last forever, and nothing can stop it." Repeat it over and over.

Tell God, "I am sorry for saying things that actively worked against what you wanted to do in my life, and thank you for blessing me beyond my wildest imagination."

THE WORDS OF GOD

The Hebrew people eventually figured things out and transformed from a slave population to a geopolitical superpower. To use a developmental psychology framework, they went from utter dependence, like that of infants, in Egypt to a more mature, collaborative phase in Canaan.

How we raise our children models and mirrors this. My son is two years old. He can not do much for himself. As his parents, my wife and I have to find him food, prepare it, and put it in front of him. If we don't, he will cry. We have to change his diaper, because he doesn't yet know how to use the toilet. At this stage, he could not survive without us. Our job as parents is to teach our kids how to eventually be self-sufficient. I will eventually transition from making all the decisions for my children to teaching them how to make their own the right way. Over time, they will step into their own identities and establish their spheres of influence.

This is a pattern you also see in Scripture. When God brought the Israelites out of Egypt, or later out of Babylonian captivity, or even later to free them from the Midianites, they were completely dependent on him. They could do nothing because their own power was limited. In return, God expected them to take what He said and enforce it, but they failed over and over again.

The Israelites successfully followed Moses out of Egyptian slavery, but could not pass the next spiritual test. They could not find the faith to overcome fear and walk forward, regardless of what lay ahead. Still, the Most High did not abandon them. All throughout the story, He maintained a personal investment in their development. Despite His divine faithfulness, the Israelites' struggles with their own belief continued to invite new battles.

BAAL GETS IN WHERE IT FITS IN

All the Israelites had to do was believe God would go with them and give them victory, but they wouldn't do it. Doubt and confusion got into their heads, and they walked out of their spirit and into their intellects.

The Israelites were eventually successful in taking the Promised Land, but they never fully beat the gods in Canaan, and we are seeing these powers show up in everyday life, thousands of years later. Baal, god of status and money, still shapes our worship of wealth and possessions. Astarte (Ishtar) continues to distort the purity of sex and intimacy by breaking down gender identity. And Molech still promotes the sacrifice of children, albeit through modern practices like abortion and the ideologies behind certain organizations.

One of the sneakiest gods we read about in the Old Testament was Baal, the "lord of the skies," known for his ability to provide increase. If Ra, or the similar Amun-Ra, was the dominant god of the Egyptians, then Baal was the dominant god of the Canaanites, eventually eclipsing even El, a much older god from the same region.

When Jesus said, "know them by their fruit," (Matthew 7:16), He was specifically talking about prophets and teachers. He meant it as a preparatory statement for the end times. Fruit and trees are a transferable theme we can use to identify spiritual tactics. Where you find Baal, you will always find:

1. *Mammon*, the worship of money.
2. Self-reliance and the idolatry of self.

"Baal" functions as more of a title than a name, which is another attempt to mimic the nature of God. The translation from Hebrew is "lord" or "owner." It is meant to convey authority, just as "Elohim" is a general term for God and "Elohim Elyon" denotes His specific title as the Most High One.

When we study the names of God, we see titles that reflect pieces of God's personality. These titles all point back to an identifiable *King,* a position reserved for the one at the top, who has traits that are exhibited in many different types of names: Jehovah Rapha ("The *Lord* Who Heals"), El Elyon ("God Most

High"), Adonai ("Lord, Master"), and El Gibbor ("Mighty God").

This presents a microcosm of how the spiritual realm of darkness operates: they all try to mimic the true God. Imagine a desperate business owner who copies another's name and business exactly, without developing their own ideas or brand value. When a strategy relies entirely on copying and misleading people into believing you are someone you are not, you would say the operation is a scam. Baal, in this sense, represents a scam no different than a text message asking you to "call this number" after claiming there has been suspicious activity on your account.

A few weeks ago, I got a text that someone had tried to change one of my financial logins. The message read, "If this wasn't you, call this number." This has never happened to me before, and I was concerned. I called the number, and a "customer support representative" began discussing measures to secure my accounts. After about thirty minutes, things started feeling funny. They were very professional but said things that didn't quite make sense. It turned out to be a scammer, trying to get me to wire them money.

This is a classic phishing attempt designed to trick you into revealing sensitive information or sending money. It is through this type of deception that evil entities operate. Just like those fraudulent texts, Baal's operation is a deceitful imitation, lacking any genuine divine authority or original power. If they can "manufacture" a fake likeness, a certain percentage of people will trust them and get scammed out of their money. Baal and all the other gods are just like this. They might try to sound like El Elyon, but they will never be El Elyon. Their best shot is to mimic and pretend, hoping a few people will fall for them.

People mistakenly assume that scammers are dumb, but it takes a certain amount of intelligence to pull this off successfully. One of my employees, a highly intelligent individual, recently told me she was scammed out of several thousand dollars because she believed a "customer service representative" was trying to protect her cryptocurrency accounts. The ploy only worked because the scammer was also intelligent and knew how to say the right things at the right time.

At the core, Baal represented submission to any spiritual lord or master aside from the Lord of Lords and the God of Abraham, Isaac, and Jacob. It acted as a "one size fits all" title that made it difficult for the Israelites to pin down. The Israelites ended up falling for Baal worship over and over, because it was everywhere, and Baal was sneaky. We cannot assume that someone worshipped Baal simply because they were rich. It was a matter of the heart, as the heart is a reflection of your worship.

Baal promised to give people what they wanted in exchange for their hearts and worship. You see intimidation, fear, and lust as the main tactics used to position the Israelites to take the bait. One of Baal's favorite tools to use was mammon. Mammon slowly convinced the Israelites that the only way for them to move forward was to figure it out on their own, without God. Our society is programmed with this core philosophy even today.

All across the internet, I see the messages of Baal and mammon being trained into our population. How often in internet forums do people tell each other, "No one is going to save you," or another way to tell people to save themselves. Even the adage "God helps those who help themselves" translates into a philosophy of "Go figure it out and then ask God to bless it."

None of this language is substantiated by God's personality. We do not see God abandoning people who do not figure it out themselves. Similarly, we do not see God blessing people just because they figured out their own solution and ran with it.

As an entrepreneur, I am familiar with the pressures of running multiple businesses and having many people depend on me. There are times to work hard and get something done. However, when your entire life turns into a deadline, it becomes an addiction. When the only way for you to get ahead is by doing it yourself, you have an idol, and it isn't God.

A BELIEF AND AN IDOL

When my wife and I got married, we were very poor. I didn't realize it at the time, but this season positioned me perfectly to commit allegiance to my own efforts.

I remember getting on a plane to visit her family before we got engaged. I wanted to ask her father about marriage and to get his blessing. At the time, I was working at a church and was on a $17,000-per-year salary.

One of the first questions my wife's father had for me was how we would make it financially. While I don't remember all of the particulars, I remember two things: where we were, and what I said in response. We were at a small coffee store inside a supermarket when I told my future father-in-law, "I will never let your daughter be poor. I will work as many jobs as I have to and do whatever I need to do, but she will not be poor."

On the surface, this sounds like a fine thing to say. However, my personality would eventually twist and warp around it.

Some people push too hard because of greed. I was pushing because of an obligation I had made, a substitute "god" that I had manufactured and worshipped through my efforts to "not be poor." Years later, when we were making millions, I still could not stop. I wouldn't stop. Anything that did not make us money was cut from my life and my schedule.

I thought I was being a good steward and making good on my promise, but my wife wanted a husband more than she wanted my provision. Unfortunately, my god in that moment was not the God of Abraham, Isaac, and Jacob. My god was the god of increase and productivity. I could not see the forest for the trees, and had slowly whittled my life down to only include the stewardship of "more."

When my first child was born, I barely saw her or my wife. It took me three years to have a collision course with destiny and realize that I was worshipping something very different than the God of the Bible.

My decline had started innocently. I meet people like this every week at events, online, or in person. They are not greedy, law-breaking people, but they are not free. Their idols have trapped them in addiction, their words have contractually obligated them to self-reliance, and their lifestyles have become identities they do not know how to escape.

I recently spoke at a conference in Nashville on the topic of influence and perception. The talk was calibrated for people selling products like consulting or coaching. Afterward, a large man came up to me and asked to talk. As soon as he opened his mouth to ask his question, he started crying.

The man apologized and said he didn't know what was happening. I told him that it was okay and that I would wait for him. After a few minutes of him struggling to articulate his thoughts, he finally got it out. "I feel like a failure if I am not growing rapidly. What is wrong with me?"

"There is nothing wrong with you," I said immediately, "but you have taken the bait of a god who does not care about you." We talked it through, and I told him how to talk to Jesus about it. His emotions, I explained, would shift once he heard what Jesus thought of him. This is always how it works. You cannot hear the words of Yeshua and not be changed by them.

I wish I had someone sit me down in 2015 or 2016 and say, "Listen, God actually wants to help and partner with you, but you are too busy partnering with yourself." Unfortunately, this perspective is not standard teaching in most churches.

Baal tells you that the only way to get ahead is if you do it for yourself. The Israelites fell for this trick before they even got to the Promised Land. While Moses is up on the mountain hearing from God, the people become unsettled and afraid. They wanted a new way to communicate with divinity. They wanted to control it. They built a golden calf and began to worship it.

Like me, you may have been taught that the Israelites were trying to create their own god. This is not expressly true. They thought Moses might have died and doubted whether he would ever come back. In their *fear*, they tried to build a new way to represent Yahweh and communicate with Him through it. They needed a version of God that they could control, and the golden calf was their solution. In fact, they gave this golden calf the credit for what Yahweh did for them in the Exodus.

In Exodus 32:4, the Israelites said, "This is your god, O Israel, who brought you up out of Egypt." They built something they could control and tried to say that it was El Elyon all along, giving Him credit for it through their new idol. It was a fabrication, performed with decent enough intentions.

Whenever you take matters into your own hands and then tell everyone that God has done it, you are following in the footsteps of the Israelites. Ironically enough, Baal was represented as a bull. What is a bull before it is fully grown? A calf. The Israelites did not meet Baal for the first time when they got to Egypt. They played with this deity in the desert. It starts when you are young and follows you through transferable bondage as an adult.

For a deeper exploration of this concept, you can find a video titled "The Altar of Baal" on my YouTube channel. For now, all you need to understand is how Baal operates, which is crucial to understanding how he fights.

HOW BAAL FIGHTS

Everything we see in the physical realm is a modified copy of the spiritual realm, and one of the more fascinating subjects in the spiritual realm is the study of altars, precisely because they reveal how spiritual forces gain influence even where our sovereignty should protect us.

In Rome, there is a 6.5-acre plot of land reserved for the United States to conduct business. This building is granted special protections under international law and is known as "inviolable," meaning that the host authorities cannot enter without explicit permission. An American visiting Italy can enter the embassy, but access for anyone else requires permission.

Legally, nothing can happen in Italy without the Italian government's awareness. However, within the embassy, all bets are off. An altar is similar.

Your mind, body, soul, and spirit are all legally off-limits. For something to occur to you, a few things must also be intact. One, you must be aware, or have granted permission that bypasses the need for awareness. Two, you must be able to change it. Three, you must retain some semblance of sovereignty pertaining to matters of your destiny. In other words, the spiritual forces of darkness cannot just kill you and be done with it.

An altar, however, carves out a small part of your life that can be affected without going through the proper chain of command. Numerous online resources delve into this subject. I recommend the work of Joshua Selman on altars, Isi Igenegba's bloodline series, and Kevin LA Ewing's studies on evil altars and spiritual warfare. These individuals have extensively documented their research, supporting it with Scripture and detailed explanations of concepts I am only briefly introducing here.

Altars can also be generational. They are the epitome of transferable bondage. This is why I tell people that whatever you do not deal with in your lifetime will be inherited by your children to be dealt with in theirs.

In the Old Testament, altars were agreements, beliefs, and physical locations. The Hebrew word for "altar" is linked to the Hebrew word for "table." In present times, we do not require a physical location for an altar to be powered, but we do need a table, or a place you eat from, in the metaphysical sense.

The best way to track down an altar you have created is, therefore, to look at where you are getting your sustenance. This topic goes very deep, and I will not cover generational altars or bloodline altars here. However, whenever a pattern shows up again and again, and you cannot figure out what is causing it, the root cause can often be traced to the presence of an altar.

When it comes to Western notions of success, we are particularly vulnerable to the altar of Baal, given how deeply ingrained its principles are from childhood. At what moment did you believe that your future was entirely up to and dependent on you? At what point did you first feel afraid that you would not have enough? And then, at what point did you control that fear by going out and making everything happen for yourself?

A person can operate for many years by worshipping the idol of production at the altar of Baal. This can bring great treasures into your life. If the altar of Baal offered no benefits, it would not be an effective trap. Yet the provision of Yahweh is far superior to any other god, spirit, or deity. It is also far greater than the provision of man. Baal does not always need you to worship it. It wins if it can get you to worship yourself.

Luckily, there are ways to fix this before we get trapped in it. Unfortunately, you must remain on guard. The heart is cunning, and it will be a central player in not only gaining your freedom but keeping it.

BREAKING THE ALTAR OF BAAL

In the Old Testament, altars were not just piles of stones but spiritual gateways represented by physical places. These altars embodied spiritual systems that could control or influence the physical realm. There are Godly altars and evil altars.

Many of the good altars were built as acts of worship. For example, in Genesis 8:20, Noah built one when they exited the ark after his family was saved. Jacob built an altar at Bethel after he had his vision of the ladder reaching to heaven. The story of Jacob is a poignant example of how altars can influence real-life events.

Many years before Jacob had his vision at Bethel, Abraham had already built an altar in the same province. Genesis 12:8 tells us, "After that, Abram traveled south and set up camp in the hill country, with Bethel to the west and Ai to the east. There he built another altar and dedicated it to the Lord, and he worshiped the Lord."

The altar Abraham built is likely a key reason why Jacob had his vision of angels ascending and descending from heaven in the same location. In response, Jacob built another altar, renewing and perpetuating the connection to the spiritual system that had already been established.

Moses built an altar at the base of Mount Sinai, and Joshua built one on Mount Ebal after entering the Promised Land. It is odd that altars show up so frequently in Scripture and yet are talked about so little when we discuss spiritual matters.

Today, an altar is less of a physical marker and more of an indication of what kinds of activities are allowed to operate. While an altar can still be tied to a physical location, it no longer depends on one. Jesus emphasized that true worship no longer required a specific geographic location but was to be expressed from the heart (John 4:21–24). What once required a physical altar or temple is now "walking around in hearts."

Can unsaved people use altars? They did in the Bible. There are spiritual systems like generosity and forgiveness that will activate, whether a person is a born-again Christian or not. Just like eating healthy food will improve your body, whether you believe in Jesus or not, these principles work because they reflect how the Most High God created everything. All systems start in the spirit, and then govern what is of the flesh. Generosity works for unsaved people because it activates a system. Forgiveness works similarly.

Not all systems are so easily powered. Some altars are required to be broken completely before any other system will be allowed jurisdiction to operate. The altar of Baal is one such altar. It is not our behavior that rejects the altar of Baal and accepts the provision of the Lord. This altar can only be broken with the mercy of the One True God. As He was necessary in the breaking out of the Israelites from the governance of the Egyptian deities, He is once again needed to break us out of the system of worship, attachment, and dependence upon the altar of Baal.

Many Christians are held subservient to the provision of mammon because they do not even know they are worshipping at the wrong altar. Your heart can be good and pleasing to God, and you can be praying for help. However, if an evil altar is running the machinery of your life, then all sorts of spiritual adversaries have access to you. Your embassy is wide open.

The principle works both ways. An unsaved business leader with an altar of generosity, powered by giving, might see systemic multiplication in their lives, because an altar is powering it.

Imagine we have a Christian business owner who loves the Lord, but is afraid of being poor. They begin to work too hard and trade away their freedom to advance. It is difficult to be obedient, give, or make sacrifices, because if it doesn't make them money, they feel emotionally compromised. Every decision is run through a filter of "Will this make me profitable? Will this bring me an increase?" If it doesn't, it is disqualified.

The decision-maker is no longer thinking, *What does God say?* but rather, *What do I say?* Through this, they do experience an increase, but it's not coming from obedience to God. It is completely disconnected from the provision of the Lord and connected exclusively to their self-effort. The consequences are tangible. They begin to feel depleted, exhausted, and behind. Not because they are poor, but because they only consider how much farther ahead they could be. This is an altar.

Their sacrifice to the altar is the very freedom that God promises. They surrender rest, trust, and spiritual clarity in exchange for the illusion of control and success. People often justify this loss through logic and their good intentions. They desire to work hard, do good things, and not want handouts, which are all virtuous. However, they stopped depending on God for his direction or His provision.

The man or woman stuck in this loop is tending to an altar by feeding it energy and sacrificing their lives to sustain it. The power behind the system here will almost always be connected to Baal. This path may lead individuals to a short-term increase, but long-term destruction.

Now, consider a business owner who trusts God. He or she knows they are designed to work diligently and allow God to bless them. They know that their profit and progress are tied to their obedience. They are called to be skillful, as we all are, but they are not confused about where their provision comes from. They personify Psalm 127:1, where the Psalmist writes, "Unless the Lord builds the house, those who build it labor in vain." They are partners in what God is building, but do not have the final say.

Every time this business owner receives income, they take a part of it and give it to someone who needs it, even if it may not always fit their budget. God honors obedience, and progress is connected to it. They are not taking it on themselves to disobey God and try to get ahead on their own efforts.

Over time, this business owner might experience ups and downs as we all do, but will somehow always become more fruitful. During good economies and bad economies, they not only survive but are somehow always thriving.

This person is also tending an altar. Psalm 1:3 says of these people, "They are like trees planted along a riverbank, bearing fruit in *every* season" (Ps. 1:3). The business owner in this example is close to the source, which allows them to produce in every season. Their sacrifice is different than the first example. Their behavior may appear to lead to short-term loss, because giving sacrificially feels difficult in the moment. However, over the long term, it always leads to life and life to the fullest.

So what do we do when we are powering the wrong altars? We want to break them and then replace them. The altar of Baal, powered by the worship of our own production, sustains many Christians, even those who are Bible-believing and born-again. You cannot break this without God's mercy, but you also will not survive without a superior altar to replace it.

In a later chapter, we will talk about the altar of generosity. In this chapter, we will explore the keys to breaking our dependence on self and creating dependence on Yahweh.

GOD AS PROVIDER

Breaking an altar is only the beginning. The empty space must be filled with something beautiful and life-giving, or the demolition will have been merely destructive, rather than transformative.

This is why understanding God as the provider is not simply a theological concept. It is the essential replacement system that must occupy the newly cleared space. The Israelites struggled with this transition. They had such a complex relationship with the concept of lordship that, at one point, God had to intervene directly to correct their understanding.

He literally tells them all to stop calling Him "Baali," which was a popular title for Yahweh at one point. "Baali" means "my lord," but Baal was so pervasive in Canaanite culture that the Israelites confused the names and fell for the bait of a counterfeit in the ways they perceived Yahweh.

As recorded in Hosea 2:16 (HCSB), the Lord declares: "In that day—this is the LORD's declaration—you will call Me, 'My husband,' and no longer call Me, 'My Baal.'" This passage (literally "my Baal"; NIV, "my master") suggests that Israel may have substituted Baal for Yahweh, attempting to conceive of Yahweh as Baal, even calling Him by this heathen name.

Here, we see the Most High God requesting His people to switch away from transactional spirituality. I don't believe the Israelites were legitimately attempting to worship Baal. They were attempting to worship God in a way that made sense to them, but it was not how He wanted to be worshiped. This kept happening because it is how all the other cultures worshipped their deities.

God wanted to be a covenant partner, not a genie in a bottle. However, because the Israelites had no roadmap for it, they defaulted to how everyone else was worshipping. If this sounds familiar, that is because we see this same religious outlook on God the Father in Western Christianity, right now in the present.

How do you know if you are operating in the right paradigm within your relationship with God? If it is so easy to fall into the trap of the wrong altar, how can you ever know if you are safe? Luckily, some signals will alert us when we are slipping towards an inferior altar, allowing interference into our lives.

The first warning sign is disbelief. If you were to shout to the heavens, calling God a liar and a coward, that would be rightly frowned upon. Other Christians would tell you that you have sinned and need to repent. Yet, in our hearts, whenever we do not believe what God has said, we are already guilty of that same disbelief.

It is not like God cannot read your heart. In fact, He is the only one who can. We commit errors when we allow ourselves to continue on in disbelief without repentance. In Romans 11 we read, "But what is God's response to him? 'I have kept for myself seven thousand men who have not bowed the knee to Baal.' So too then, at the present time, there has come to be a remnant [a small *believing* minority] according to God's gracious choice" (Rom. 11:4–5).

A small, *believing* minority. The only time you will find yourself falling into self-reliance and the worship of production is when you do not believe what God has said about your allocated provision from Him. The Israelites validated this. They would get to the edge of the promised land after seeing God do crazy miracles, and they didn't believe what He said about them and about their future. They chose to believe what they saw and not to believe what God said. We can, and should, link this disbelief to all the times they fell for Baal worship later on.

When you are struggling to believe what God says about your future, there are spiritual systems at work attempting to corrupt you. The enemy and his organized system of destruction want you to place your trust in anything but God. This is a signature ingredient of the altar of Baal: if people do not believe God, they must fend for themselves.

The second warning sign is an overreliance on carnal systems of governance, on yourself, and on the pursuit of self-enrichment. Baal will attempt to divert your trust in God and cause you to place that trust in yourself or in your system of intellectual control. This often happens when legitimate circumstances cause you to feel weak or vulnerable.

I feel sad when I hear people say they believe in God totally, but then go out into the world talking about how bad everything is and how we need to prepare for it. These individuals have an altar in their lives that provides for them, and it is not a Godly one.

The altar of Baal only functions when you are not aware of it. When I began to study all of this, my first thought was not, "Good thing I am not feeding an altar of Baal in my life." My first thought was, "God, please forgive me and show me mercy, and reveal anywhere I have been feeding off a counterfeit altar." The Holy Spirit showed me several areas that I could not see, and I broke them down and repented of them.

Watch out when you become consumed with who the president is, or what's going to happen if "XYZ" doesn't happen just right. It is a temptation to feed the altar of self-protection and self-reliance, both of which are squarely in Baal's territory. While these things are important, you must slow down when you notice them become all-consuming. If it is so important to you that it is creating fear, you are being set up to compromise somewhere.

The third warning sign is sexual promiscuity or misconduct. The most popular form of Baal worship from the days of Moses, Joshua, and Gideon was sexual promiscuity performed in front of a physical altar. I have found sexual promiscuity to be one of the main things that breaks down a person's discernment in the spiritual realm. It is the opposite of fasting and extended prayer, which extend spiritual discernment. An overindulgence in the desires of the flesh can blind you to any realm except the physical.

CRITICAL JUNCTURES

There are two main times in a person's journey when Baal and self-reliance attempt to swoop in and redirect our trust in God's sovereignty. One is when the person is weak and in need of saving. The other is when they are suddenly very strong and enjoying their victory. These are the two polar extremes of the experience.

The difference between the altar of salvation and the altar of Baal, besides the eternal ramifications, is simple: Who is saving you? Are you saving yourself, or is God saving you? Are you defending yourself, or is God defending you?

One time, I was on a prayer walk discussing several pressing issues with the King of the Ages. I sometimes forget how big He is because He is my father, and I have been guilty of taking for granted my time with Him. In this instance, I was asking Him to fix a certain issue, and He told me why it was not being handled. "I can fix the issue, but you are too busy fixing it yourself. I will wait until you are done."

That was a wake-up call, and I repented for my lack of belief. One way to remove the confines of the altar of Baal from your thinking is to realize that there is a God who is personally interested in you. Your responsibility is to partner with Him and do what He says.

Many believers who fall prey to this altar do so because of money. At some point along their journey, they started to believe that money could save them. To open up the trust necessary for God's provision, we have to first deal with this false altar.

MAMMON, ANOTHER COUNTERFEIT

Inside the land of Canaan, there was a city called Tyre. The inhibitors were materialistic and greedy. The Greeks called the people of Tyre the "Phoenicians." The Phoenicians were obsessed with money, possessions, and status. This was the land of Baal, and people were bound to their altars to grow in wealth.

The entire economic center of Tyre was based on trade, so competing for wealth was normal. You got ahead through what you were able to accumulate through commerce. Entire outposts were set up and funded through the buying and selling of slaves, specifically Israelite slaves.

Later on in the story, God gets very angry with Tyre. In Ezekiel, we read, "Tyre is like a ship that will be caught in a tempest and sunk with total loss of cargo and crew." What could make God so angry? Was it that they were selling His people as slaves? That would make sense, wouldn't it? But that is not what triggered this judgment from God. I do not believe God was happy that they were selling Israelite slaves, but that isn't what caused the vindictive judgment from the Most High.

God's problem with Tyre was much more precise and far more terrifying because it was a sin any of us could be guilty of committing. In Ezekiel 28:5, the root of God's anger is discovered: "By your great wisdom and by your trade, you have increased your riches and power, and your heart is proud and arrogant because of your wealth" (Ezek. 28:5).

Tyre's judgment applies to us in the present. When we find our hearts becoming arrogant because of our wealth, we are participating in the same behavior that led God to desire to sink an entire city of people like a ship in the ocean.

The people of Tyre worshipped their own competency. They thought, "We are better because we make more money." They ultimately suffered judgment because they reveled in their ability to provide for themselves. God has a habit of judging what is inside a man's heart, and I do not want God to ever see the same spiritual condition of Tyre in my own heart.

Unfortunately, the poorer a society becomes, the easier it is for it to be seduced by the same gods that enticed the Israelites. The education systems in America and the church have not taught people what Godly prosperity looks like. This leaves us in a vulnerable position where people don't know how to live in abundance without turning to the spirit of mammon or the altar of Baal.

I meet these people almost every week at business conferences. They are trying to get ahead and break free from financial constraints. There is nothing inherently wrong with wanting to get ahead, but their misguided education has led them to become obsessed with accumulating, hoarding, and stressing over money. These sacrifices cut off the Godly altars in their lives and feed the evil altars attached to the wrong deities. These individuals remain in bondage to the spiritual systems of Baal, never in poverty, but never fully prosperous, either.

We cannot, however, use this as a logical reason to avoid any desire for money. In fact, that makes it worse. If you were to starve yourself for 100 days, your desire for food would be off the charts, which can actually increase your hunger for, well, *increase*.

Fasting is effective as a spiritual tool and a physiological tool in small doses. Fasting for the body mirrors generosity for your financial life. Some of the places I see the altar of Baal most at work include places where people were raised to believe that God wants them to be poor.

When you limit yourself to poverty, you open yourself up tenfold to the temptation and seduction of Baal. The best defense is Godly provision and adherence to God's instructions, which includes repentance, generosity, and Godly thinking.

Mammon is a two-sided coin. Your master is what you worship, and many in the church are worshipping poverty as much as the world is worshipping money. Fortunately, God is not a judge in heaven waiting to penalize you for your instincts. You don't have to be afraid of Him, even if you make mistakes.

The one thing we cannot do, however, is pendulum swing. Nor can we take His mercy for granted. Wealth gained apart from the backing of the Lord will always lead to sorrow. The worship of money is a portal to all sorts of problems in your life. Breaking free from such deeply ingrained altars can be one of the hardest things we do in this life.

BREAKING THE ALTAR

God led me through a series of steps when He showed me my areas of self-reliance. I told you that when I first discovered this, my first response was to repent and ask God to show me where I had unknowingly been powering the altar of Baal in my life. The Holy Spirit loves to counsel us, so He did just that.

I began to untangle the web of confusion and lies around my finances. The first step was repentance. The second step was renunciation and rejection. The third step was to relinquish. And the final step was to request and replace. If you want to use the following prayers on your own time, you can do so.

Repentance

"God, I repent for allowing this into my life. I want to change my mind and how I think about this area, specifically about provision. I ask for mercy to cover the transactions that took place to feed this altar and keep it going without my understanding."

Renunciation and Rejection

"God, I renounce and reject this altar and this system. I reject any sustenance or provision that has come as a result of this belief system and this altar. I no longer want to eat from this table; I want to eat the food from the table of the Lord. I reject the provision of this altar and I choose the provision of the Lord, the Most High God, the One who provides for me."

Relinquish

"Father, I relinquish control and ownership over anything that you do not want me to have. If there are finances, positions, spheres of influence, or protections that are not from You, I relinquish them. I ask to trade them all for the finances, positions, and spheres of influence that come complete with the promise and the backing of Yahweh. I let go of anything that is not in Your will for me. Please tell me if there is anything I am supposed to let go of and how I am supposed to do it."

Request and Replace

"God, your name is Jehovah Jirah, you are the greatest provider that exists. I ask You to provide for me. As I let go of the provision from anything that I have manufactured, any counterfeit altar of sustenance, I request for You to become my provider and take care of me. I know that You will always supply all of my needs. And I don't have to be afraid of anything, ever again. Thank you."

BELIEF SYSTEMS AND POWER

"For as he thinketh in his heart, so is he"
    —*Prov. 23:7.*

Your brain is equipped with programming functionality that can be used to imprint the future with your desired outcomes.[1] Our minds are the most advanced computational devices on earth. It is not only a computational device, but the raw firepower that the human brain possesses to create is unrivaled. Most of the brain's features are so advanced that we do not even know how to use them.

Imagine you have the first-generation iPhone from 2007. If you tried to use that phone today, the hardware would not be able to run a modern iOS. Most of the business owners I work with are all looking for more output, better performance, and higher functionality. They mistakenly assume that the highest-leverage area to improve is their hardware, but this is rarely the case.

Now imagine you have a brand-new, just-released iPhone complete with the most advanced technology on the planet. However, you are running that iPhone with software from the original iPhone in 2007. It would work, sort of, but it won't be able to do most of what the hardware can do. The software is too outdated and will never be able to take advantage of the more advanced processors and hardware capacity.

The hardware of our brains works similarly. You can think of our thoughts as the software that controls how much utility we get from the brain. Then add to this mix the integration component that connects us to a spiritual dimension.

If we are coded correctly, we have the capacity to weave multiple dimensions of reality: the physical, the emotional, and the spiritual. We can harness the predictive nature of the Spirit, organize it in the data hub of our emotional and logical centers, and then act on it (choice) in the physical realm.

We can also prevent mistakes and regrets before they happen. We can receive counsel from the Holy Spirit on how we speak, interact, and make decisions. It does not matter if you believe this or not, just as it would not matter if you believed in the Sun. It is there, and operates autonomously from your belief. What is determined by your belief is not whether it is real, but whether you can harness it.

The mind, comprised of two hemispheres, is a portal that can connect us to the collective data from all around us. We are constantly integrating this information without realizing it, but most people cannot organize it because they are unaware that the integration is even happening.

Every legitimate human has a spirit, a body, and a soul component, which includes the mind, will, and emotions. We can organize these loosely into three different realms: the first realm (the physical), the second realm (the soul realm of the mind, will, and emotions), and the third realm (the spirit). When scientists refer to terms like collective consciousness or quantum entanglement, they are attempting to bring order to the way the third realm (the spirit) connects all things together.

Popular success psychology (often referred to as "pop psychology") has done a massive disservice to the human condition by teaching people to suppress and ignore their feelings. Our feelings act as decoding mechanisms to decipher the realm of the third heaven. This is why Paul writes, "Peace is the umpire [or ruler]" (Col. 3:15), to be used when making decisions. Peace can be defined as a regulated physiological state that starts in the mind and works its way into the body.

When a person feels peace, they often experience:

- Low sympathetic activation (no fight-or-flight or jittery feelings in the body)
- High parasympathetic activity (restful, calm nervous system)
- Alpha and theta brainwave rhythms (reflective, calm)
- Reduced cortisol and adrenaline (neurochemical activity shifts towards safety, even amid chaos)
- Increased serotonin (a calm, steady confidence)

Many of these are indicated by how you feel. While some pastors say, "It doesn't matter how you feel," this perspective can be misleading. Fear, for instance, is a feeling that creates a physiological response. God constantly instructs us not to experience it.

It does matter how you feel because how you feel determines which realm you're getting your instructions from. A person only getting their instructions from the first and second heavens (the physical and the soul realms) will feel afraid a lot. A person getting their instructions from the spiritual realm (the third heaven) will feel secure, steady, and grounded, even if told to run or to fight.

I want to get us to a point where we are grateful for the capacity God has given us to process His voice and the information in all three realms. We were, after all, placed on earth to act as governors. To do that, we need access to the information in the third realm, specifically to access the guidance of heaven.

We have been given the most incredible asset to communicate with God and walk in our authority. Every day, our minds organize terabytes of information into short and long-term memory banks. The mind uses these memory banks to develop heuristics that give us clues about what to do and when to do it. Our split-second decisions get smarter and smarter as we reconcile old data with new goals, a process called "thin-slicing."[2]

The enemy knows all of this, and he is cunning. It is therefore essential to understand what is going on inside our minds and remove anything blocking our ability to hear from God and walk in His promises. It is not enough to possess a mind, which you obviously have. We must ensure the software of the mind (our beliefs and thoughts) match the thoughts and promises of God.

ALIGNING BELIEFS WITH SCRIPTURE

Throughout the Bible, it is clear that God is after our beliefs more than He is trying to change our circumstances. That is because our beliefs influence our circumstances. Our circumstances were never supposed to influence our beliefs, and that is often the trap.

It is why the Israelites failed the first time they tried to take the Promised Land. It is the reason people did not pray and stand in faith for things. It is the reason Joseph's brothers tried to kill him. It is the reason King Saul fell from power and needed David to replace him.

When we forget what God said and instead put our faith in our circumstances, we allow the circumstances to rule us. When this happens, we are more easily swayed to turn to counterfeit gods and deities to help us fix it. In the mind, this shows up as cognitive dissonance and cognitive distortion.

When there is a gap between what we believe and what we experience, a painful psychological fissure is created. The mind struggles to reconcile two conflicting pieces of data. In many cases, people choose to lower their expectations to match their experiences. It might feel bad to live a life below your potential, but it feels less painful in the moment than experiencing the dissonance.

Whenever cognitive dissonance occurs, even if we refuse to let go of a particular promise, our minds are capable of creating two beliefs at the same time. The easiest thing to do is to lower our expectations to match whatever we are seeing. When this happens, our words, beliefs, and expectations will all pivot around a circumstance. This is what the Israelites did when they first encountered the giants of Canaan. There was absolutely no faith in God. They said, "This was stupid. We are going to die, and we must go back to Egypt."

In the short term, it feels more painful to hang on to God and wait for our circumstances to come around than it is to just let go of our faith. However, this is what Scripture instructs us to do.

Now, what about when you refuse to let go of what God promised you, but are not quite certain that He will actually, really accomplish it? Again, the mind can create two conflicting beliefs at the same time. King David dealt with this, as did Moses. This dilemma is part of how the mind operates, and one of the hardest quandaries to reconcile.

One of my mentors recently asked me, "Do you know what the main problem with David was?" I responded honestly that I didn't know. He replied, "King David had the faith to take down Goliath, but he didn't have the identity to possess all of Israel. God had to teach him identity before he could fully promote him." His conjecture is supported by Scripture and is precisely why a lot of strong Christians experience hardship today.

Your beliefs stack up on top of each other to create your identity. Moses, who the Bible says was a powerful speaker, could not get past his insecurity and shame, so God had to raise up another to speak for him.

What happens when two beliefs creep up and exist right next to each other? One belief says, "God will do this. He can do it. You are called to do it." Another belief says, "Maybe He can, but He won't. I am not capable. I messed up. I am going to fail." This is called value conflict, a byproduct of cognitive dissonance, and almost always results in self-sabotage.

I've had many deliverance moments in my life, and I am always amazed at how simple it is to resolve. Often, we think the devil is obstructing us and blocking us, only to realize that the devil isn't even there anymore. Years ago, a situation may have been orchestrated to create a belief that was not from God, and years later, the residue of that belief will still be acting to cause self-sabotage.

The great news for us is that there is not a single person in Scripture who did not have to learn to depend on what God said about them, and to replace a lie with a promise.

Every person has wrestled with identity issues, insecurity, and self-esteem. In almost every case, the true block was not what they believed or didn't believe about God, but what they believed about themselves. If there is anything you believe about yourself that contradicts what God believes about you, you must repent for it, and ask God to help you change your mind.

When we carry conflicting values and conflicting beliefs, the mind plays tug-of-war with itself. This is where shame is created. Neurochemically, shame is a unique phenomenon in which the mind begins "self-evaluating"and finds itself to be lacking.

SHAME AND ALIGNMENT

Ryan Bush, author of *Designing the Mind*, writes, "A special part of your brain is always watching you, constantly making evaluations, and dynamically delivering chemicals based on those evaluations. These chemicals are responsible for your mood."[3]

Our achievements, and the feelings they create in the mind, have less to do with the size or scope of the achievement itself and much more to do with what they tell us about ourselves.

Albert Bandura's work on observational learning and modeling[4] explains that our actions generate value by showing that we possess the traits we value in others. This is mirrored in the financial markets and the world of business. When you own a business, the goal is always to create and steward its "market value." Tim Koller writes, "Companies exist to meet customer needs in a way that translates into reliable returns to investors."[5] The market value of a company is determined by how reliably it does these two things: (a) meets the needs of the customer, and (b) creates reliable returns to investors. But what about the value of a human being?

Psychologically speaking, our most rewarding experiences will always align with our assessment of our personal values, not our "net worth" from a monetary standpoint, but our "net personal value" from an alignment standpoint.[6]

If, at any point, we feel that we are not in alignment with who we want to be, we will sabotage ourselves to return to our most recent point of alignment.[7] Once again, we see conflicting beliefs at work.

A belief is a complex thing because it pertains not just to the past, but also to the present and the future. If you have lived a life of struggle, pain, and misery, your belief systems are likely telling you to expect more struggle, pain, and misery from your future. This belief then forces you to experience even more struggle, pain, and misery, so that you feel like you are valuable. That is how value is created. When we align our circumstances with what we expect, we reinforce our value to ourselves and to others.

Brianna Wiest, author of *The Mountain Is You*, explains, "If there is an ongoing gap between where you are and where you want to be—and your efforts to close it are consistently met with your own resistance, pain, and discomfort—self-sabotage is almost always at work."[8] If, at any point, we feel that we are *not* in alignment with who we want to be, we will sabotage ourselves to return to our most recent point of alignment.[9]

The reason many Christians struggle in their lives, financially and otherwise, is not because they do not have enough support. It is because they have developed beliefs that tell them they are supposed to struggle. Struggling and suffering are very different. There are some places we can only get to spiritually through suffering. Jesus was not called a "Man of Sorrows" for no reason (see Isaiah 53:3), but suffering for suffering's sake is childish and irresponsible.

I see many churches today that lack power because they have placed more value on suffering than they have on destroying the powers of darkness and advancing the kingdom of heaven. The terms "prosper" and "prosperous" are found dozens of times throughout Scripture, always linked to obedience as a divine promise.

Unfortunately, our minds will never allow us to prosper if our identities are shaped by a belief system that promotes suffering as a universal, inescapable law that we must constantly endure.

Our values, which come from our beliefs, are the key drivers that cause us to behave in specific ways. Even when we do not understand why we are acting or feeling a certain way, our values drive the subconscious towards a goal of fulfilling that value in real life.

Most of the current landscape of self-help curriculum does not work. That is not a judgment against the competency of the teachers. It is simply an assessment based on observational experience. If I were to take you through a process of making your goals bigger without first addressing your beliefs about

God, about yourself, about the world, it would create nothing more than self-sabotage and glass ceilings.

HEMISPHERES OF THE BRAIN

To fully utilize the tools in this chapter, we have to give our intellects enough breathing room to design, but without letting them take over. Ian McGilchrist, author of *The Matter With Things*, has done groundbreaking research on the brain's two hemispheres and how they support different cognitive functions. He writes, "The left hemisphere's world is a virtual one, whereas the right hemisphere's world is the real world."

McGilchrist calls the right hemisphere the "ruler," and the left hemisphere the "emissary." The left hemisphere is where rigid, "logical" thinking comes from, while everything in the left hemisphere is a re-interpretation of the images extracted from the right hemisphere.

"I believe that nowadays we live no longer in the presence of the world, but rather in a re-presentation of it. The significance of that is that the left hemisphere's task is to 're-present' what first 'presents' to the right hemisphere. This re-presentation has all the qualities of a virtual image: an infinitely thin, immobile, fragment of a vast, seamless, living, ever-flowing whole. From a standpoint within the representation, everything is reversed. Instead of seeing what is truly present as primary, and the representation as a necessarily diminished derivative of it, we see reality as merely

a special case of our representation – one in which something is added in to 'animate' it."
—Ian McGilchrist

The implications of McGilchrist's work are backed up by modern neuroscience research. For instance, patients with right-hemisphere brain damage often struggle to recognize familiar faces or understand context in social settings. Patients with damage in the left hemisphere, on the other hand, often have difficulty with language and spelling, but their broad understanding of their environment remains intact.

Consider the brain's left hemisphere as an automobile, comprising a combination of cables, pieces, and parts. The right hemisphere operates as the designer and engineer. The right hemisphere sees all possibilities. It creates without limitation or constraint. However, we must relearn how to use it and trust it if we are to advance.

These hemispheric differences are not just interesting in neuroscience. The engineering reveals how God designed us to interface with both physical and spiritual realities simultaneously. The left hemisphere's analytical precision and the right hemisphere's holistic vision are not competing systems. In fact, they are designed to work in harmony.

Understanding this design helps us grasp how our minds were created to receive revelation and implement it in the natural world. However, this system requires fuel to function optimally. Just as a high-performance vehicle needs the right fuel mixture to achieve its potential, our brains, and particularly the visionary right hemisphere, require specific spiritual and neurological fuel to operate as God intended.

This fuel source is not remotely mysterious or inaccessible. It is something most of us use constantly, often without realizing its power. The fuel that powers this divine interface is something deceptively simple, yet profound: attention.

THE FUEL SOURCE OF IMAGINATION

A lot of my work was built on the shoulders of giants, including Tony Robbins, Jim Rohn, and spiritual leaders and teachers from the last 3,000 years. If you have studied self-help curriculum before, you have likely heard this statement attributed to Tony Robbins: "Where focus goes, energy flows."

Attention is the fuel source that allocates functionality to the different parts of our brain. Although small in physical scope, your brain comprises a massive surface area of special activity. There are over 100 billion different nerve cells all clustered together in a surface area of about 350 square inches.[10]

Scientists call these nerve cells neurons, and they are arranged in a giant highway of connection points. Each neuron can connect and disconnect from other nerve cells, with the potential for an astonishing range of 1,000 to 50,000 connections per cell, multiplied by 100 billion cells.[11] We are talking trillions of connections. That is why your hardware (the brain) can process thoughts (software activation) so quickly. Most of this processing is done without you even thinking about it.

Of the 60,000 or so thoughts going through your mind every day, most of them are repeats from the day before. Scientists suggest that up to 70 percent of your thoughts are buried in routine programs that you did not even know existed.[12] You will not become aware of them until your attention happens to land on it.

Attention is a complicated subject. It serves to "light up" the different connections in your brain, but it is not in and of itself a "connection." Attention is not a thought. It merely fuels or lights up the thought.[13] McGilchrist addresses the complexity when he writes, "Attention is not just another 'function' alongside other cognitive functions. Its ontological status is of something prior to function."

In the movie *Inside Out*, we see a panel of workers inside Riley Anderson's brain, each representing an emotion or a neurochemical function. Imagine if every thought or connection in your brain were a little worker. Your attention acts like a flashlight. When it shines on a thought, that thought becomes active and real. Until then, it exists only as a possibility.

One reason meditation has been gaining popularity is that it works like a flashlight, revealing possibilities within a person's subconscious. Once you see a thought, you can deal with it. That might mean that you release and let it go, or empower the thought by thinking about it more. The more you think about something, the stronger the neural pathways become, forming a kind of mental GPS that helps you return to that thought more easily.

BAD NEURAL PATHWAYS

Our brains can (and do) create neural pathways that cause repeated thoughts and emotions that we don't want to have. If you are in a bad car wreck, your software might map an association between driving and extreme pain. If you give a speech and it does not go well, you might develop a fear of getting in front of people again. The more you avoid looking at the painful neural connection, the longer and more stubbornly it stays in place, and the more entrenched other systems become around it.

Remapping this connection requires having a new memory to overwrite the old association. The good news is that this mapping can be done whether you experience the physical sensation or not. That is, you do not have to get into another car wreck to fix the association from the previous one. In a similar fashion, you can remap a painful public speech without getting up in front of people to try again.

Suppose McGilchrist is right, and the left hemisphere of the brain is simply displaying a picture from the right hemisphere of the brain. In that case, we know the brain will remap an association from the picture just as easily as it can remap from an actual experience. This insight opens the door to something powerful: the ability to reshape not only our past associations but also the direction of our lives moving forward.

CREATING THE FUTURE

The past, present, and future are different realms within the flow of information. In physics, time is a byproduct of gravity. In neuroscience, time is the filing cabinet our brains use to store and retrieve memories. Without a sense of time, that cabinet flies open, and the usual order collapses. [14]

This phenomenon isn't just theoretical. If you have been in prolonged meditative states, you may have experienced the phenomenon where time ceases to exist. In the book of Joshua, God commands his people to meditate on his law, *day and night* (Josh. 1:8). This is interesting because day and night are features of *time*. It is as if he is saying, "Meditate on this until you lose track of time."

Why is time so important to the way we function? Let's say that I ask you to meet me somewhere on Monday. Without a shared system for keeping time, that meeting would be impossible. However, this concept goes much deeper than scheduling. The brain needs a place to store information, so it can find it when it needs it. Time is one way that your brain organizes information.

The caveat is that the hemispheres use different filing cabinets, and we must understand each one in order to use them. For example, the left hemisphere of the brain attaches time to memories.[15] The right hemisphere stores memory with *context*, but without time. [16]

Most people have a bias towards one hemisphere or the other. However, you can never create the future with the left hemisphere. The capacity to imagine, to form, and to anticipate what doesn't yet exist is the domain of the right hemisphere. If we take this insight and apply it to our belief systems, there are massive implications for our spiritual and emotional lives.

For one, there is a much smaller difference between the past and the future than we realize. The future is quite literally the past that has not yet occurred. Every memory in your mind started long ago, as a *possible* future that had not yet been converted into reality. Our timekeeper, the brain's left hemisphere, is constantly "printing" something, from our future table of possibilities to our memories. We can actively participate in what this conversation looks like, and sometimes even *when* it happens.

The problem is that our hardware and software can be weaponized and used against us if we don't understand them. The enemy has studied creation for a long time and understands the way God crafted us.

Most of our anxiety about the future comes from associations that are linked to some sort of pain in our past. Whenever we don't deal with shame from our past, it will always try to project itself onto our future. The more anxious we are, the more avoidant we become. The more avoidant we are, the longer these neural pathways are left untouched, and the stronger the anxiety becomes.

The antidote is functional *teleology*, or our mind's ability to restructure itself in preparation for a desired future outcome. When we stop the avoidance, and "reprint" a better picture of our future than what we are afraid of from our past, our neurology begins to reorganize.[17] It doesn't happen in thirty seconds like a microwave. It takes time. The famous psychologist Alfred Adler described teleology as a tool that can shape the conditions *today* that are necessary to achieve breakthroughs later.[18]

However, that raises the question of what we use to create this different future, if all we have are past experiences that we do not want to repeat? We do it through the Word of God. Scripture gives us the things we are to think about and the outcomes we are to imagine. Then he instructs us to remove doubt and fear, so we can truly believe and expect to see what He has promised come to pass.

Our belief systems must come from repeated exposure to God's promises until we have the experience necessary to support them. Scripture says that faith comes by hearing, and hearing by the Word of God. This means that speaking God's promises out loud can deepen our belief. Psychological studies support this: people are more likely to believe in what they hear themselves say.[19]

In order to walk in the future God has prepared for us, we must intentionally reshape our internal narratives to fully align with His Word. This is not just a spiritual discipline; it's a neurological one. The more we engage with His promises, the more they begin to shape both our thoughts and our realities.

A LIST OF PROMISES

Almost every month, I host events across the world to take people through these concepts in detail. We practice them and allow ourselves to heal and grow past the memories that are keeping us stuck. All of it is based on the timeless principles of God's truth, further validated and substantiated by modern advances in psychology and neuroscience. We usually take two full days to break down both the scientific research and the practical application, and it often leads to all sorts of breakthroughs.

I have tried to condense a small section of what we do at these events into this chapter, but there is no way the information transfer can be performed entirely in a book. If you'd like to go deeper, you'll find a schedule of upcoming events and additional resources in the back of this book.

To make this chapter more effective, I want to leave you with a list of promises you can find in Scripture that will apply to your financial life. Speak these out loud every day and watch what starts to happen in the expectations you have for your life.

- I have the mind of Christ, and it teaches me to make godly decisions daily. The mind of Christ gives me good memory and recall; I have the ability to retain knowledge. I do not lean on my own understanding, but I possess "divine intelligence" through the mind of Christ; the mind of Christ reveals things I need to know about the future (1 Cor. 2:10–16).

- I am filled with the knowledge of God's will in all wisdom and spiritual understanding. His will is my prosperity. (Col. 1:19; Ps. 35:27).
- God has given me access to everything I need to live a good and godly life. All of my promises are "baked in," it is up to me to receive them (2 Peter 1:3).
- God delights in my prosperity. He gives me power to get wealth, that He may establish His covenant upon the earth. (Deut. 8:18; 11:12).
- I immediately respond in faith to the guidance of the Holy Spirit within me. I am always in the right place at the right time because my steps are ordered by the Lord. (Ps. 37:23).
- God has given me all things that pertain to life and godliness, and I am well able to possess all that God has provided for me. (Num. 13:30; 2 Peter 1:3–4).
- God is the unfailing, unlimited source of my supply. My financial income now increases as the blessings of the Lord overtake me. (Deut. 28:2).
- As I give, it is given unto me, good measure, pressed down, shaken together, and running over. (Luke 6:38).
- I honor the Lord with my income and my increase. Thus, every dimension of my life overflows with blessings from an uncontainable source of joy. My businesses are blessed, and my land is blessed, and everything I possess is blessed. (Prov. 3:9–10).

- I am like a *flourishing* tree planted by rivers of water. I am deeply rooted and I produce good fruit in every season. I am never dry, never tired, never fainting — *EVER BLESSED*, whatever I do PROSPERS. The grace of God even makes my mistakes prosper. (Ps. 1:3).
- The LORD will set me high above all the nations of the world. When people attack me, the LORD attacks them and conquers them; *they attack in one direction and scatter like fools in seven.* The LORD establishes me and everybody sees it. The one true God claims me; they are in awe of Him. (Deut. 28:1).
- My city is blessed because I live in it. My children are blessed. My investments, bank accounts, partnerships, and businesses are blessed. I am blessed *wherever I go and whatever I do*; the stamp of the blessing of the LORD is marked across my life and cannot be undone. The LORD has guaranteed a blessing of prosperity on *everything* I do, and I am constantly filled up with more than I need. The blessings of the Lord *find me* and overtake me in EVERY area of my life. (Deut. 28:1–14).
- I always end up *ahead, not behind, and at the top,* not the bottom. (Deut. 28:13).
- The blessing of the Lord makes a person truly rich, and He adds no sorrow with it. (Prov. 10:22).
- My God makes all grace abound toward me in every favor and earthly blessing, so that I have all sufficiency for all things and abound to every good work. (2 Cor. 9:8).
- The Lord has opened unto me His good treasure and blessed the work of my hands. He has commanded

the blessing upon me in my storehouse and all that I undertake. (Deut. 28:8,12).

- I delight myself in the Lord, who gives me my heart's desires. (Ps. 37:4).
- The Lord rebukes the devourer for my sake, and no weapon that is formed against my finances will prosper. All obstacles and hindrances to my financial prosperity are now dissolved. (Mal. 3:10,11; Isa. 54:17).
- The Word of God renews my mind; therefore, I forbid thoughts of failure and defeat to inhabit my mind. (Eph. 4:23).
- I am delivered from the power and authority of darkness. I cast down reasonings and imaginations that exalt themselves against the knowledge of God, and I bring every thought into captivity to the obedience of God's Word. (2 Cor. 10:3–5).
- I am filled with the wisdom of God, and I am led to make wise and prosperous financial decisions. The Spirit of God guides me into all truth regarding my financial affairs. (John 16:13).
- The Lord causes my thoughts to become agreeable to His will, and so my plans are established and succeed. (Prov. 16:3 [AMP]).
- There is no lack, for my God supplies all my needs according to His riches in glory by Christ Jesus. (Phil. 4:19).
- The Lord is my shepherd, and I do not want. Jesus came that I might have life and have it more abundantly. (Ps. 23:1; John 10:10).
- Having received the abundance of grace and the gift

of righteousness, I reign as a king in life by Jesus Christ. (Rom. 5:17).

- The Lord has pleasure in the prosperity of His servant, and Abraham's blessings are mine. (Ps. 35:27; Gal. 3:14).

THE ANATOMY OF FAITH

*"Faith is the confidence that what we hope for will
actually happen; it gives us assurance about things
we cannot see."*
—*Hebrews 11:1 (NLT)*

I was sitting in my "repentance" chair, arguing with God. The argument had started several days before. Something had gone poorly, and I wanted to know why. I hadn't always included the Holy Spirit in my decisions. For most of my life, I never even asked Him for an opinion. I provided for myself, worked for myself, and made decisions based on what made sense to me.

Then my life unraveled. I went through a series of significant setbacks that eventually forced me to include Him. It was not an ideal path, but sometimes this is how it happens. It's amazing how low some of us need to go before we look up.

It took me a while to learn how to hear the voice of God and decipher it from my own thoughts. Once I learned to hear the voice, however, I started listening, and I learned to trust it.

One day, I asked Him to help me, and He did. I would pray about something, hear an instruction, and go do it. Shockingly, it worked. I started to do and say things that did not make sense to me, but it continued to work. With Him, I always knew I was going to be okay. And if something happened that I could not fix, He would help me navigate it.

Now, what about when God guides you into dangerous territory, and doesn't seem to be interested in getting you out of it?

This question was what had led to my standstill with Him. Not everything in my life was better because God was directing me. He had let me fail in something, and I couldn't trust Him because he was willing to let that happen.

I was triggered over something very small. God had asked me to do something, and it had not worked out. Nobody died, I didn't go bankrupt, but it was enough to crack the door open. The way God was responding showed that it was planned to be this way.

For me, it wasn't about winning or losing, but control. In hindsight, I see that God was allowing me to get rid of a belief I had carried for a long time. The belief had been that, if God did not come through, I could always come through for myself.

I was sitting in my repentance chair, mad at God, in the middle of writing this book. Suddenly, I was not so sure I even wanted to release it at all. The situation went from bad to worse when I was asked a question by something other than the Holy Spirit. A voice spoke into my mind and asked, "Are you sure that God is a better provider than you are?"

Like so many things in the spirit, the process starts with a voice, a word, a question, and if you do not have the capacity to answer the voice the right way, you will open a door into your heart. The serpent, although studied and intelligent, has but one main strategy to dethrone the human race: doubt, as in, "Did God really say this?" (Gen. 3:1).

The voice may have belonged to a principality or a higher-ranking demon of sorts, but in the moment, it didn't matter. I was already frustrated with God, and I agreed with the question. The situation reminded me of the story of Jesus in the desert. The Bible says that he was led into the wilderness by the Spirit, and the devil knew he was hungry. Satan is not an idiot; despite his limitations, he can plan and he can think.

Satan knew Jesus had not eaten in 40 days and asked Jesus to take care of himself. The first temptation was one of reliance: "If you are the Son of God, why not tell these stones to become loaves of bread?" Matthew 4:3 (NLT). In other words, "Meet your own needs. Make something happen for yourself. Are you not hungry? Then go get some food." Satan will always tempt us to use our authority to take care of ourselves, and to replace the provision of Yahweh with that of our own effort.

Jesus' "no" was quick and to the point. He then backs it up with Scripture: "The scriptures say, 'People do not live by bread alone, but by every word that comes from the mouth of God.'"

I did not respond to my temptation the same way Jesus responded to His temptation. I thought, *Hmm. Good question. Let's consider it. I think you might have a point.* This is where the door went from a narrow crack to fully open. All it really takes is a moment of consideration, and you can tilt.

My frustration with God turned into bitterness. I remembered my life when I was providing for myself and, in some areas, had done a pretty good job. More importantly, I had control. Nobody could determine whether I had a lot or a little, I decided for myself. My tilt turned into an intense outburst of rebellion that I could not walk away from.

What is so amazing about God is that He did not respond to my rebellion with anger of His own. Through the process, He remained kind as He talked to me, though He said very little.

Proverbs 15:1 says, "A gentle answer deflects anger" (NLT). Yet the lack of an equally emotional "outburst" from Him was causing me to lose my justification. God was not defending Himself, and that made me doubt whether I was right or wrong. I found myself having to manufacture reasons to be upset, stay angry, and ultimately, walk away from trusting Him.

The kindness of God is extraordinary. Yet under the circumstances, it angered me that He could be so kind when I would act so mean. When you open your mind to the lies of the enemy. you will not be reasonable, and the effects will be felt immediately.

WHY GOD DOES WHAT HE DOES

An easy answer is simply that He is wiser and smarter than we are. However, the truth runs deeper. Everything God does is manifold, meaning He accomplishes multiple things at the same time. When God speaks, it heals us, empowers us, repositions us, corrects us, and establishes us. Correction is not linear, but rather exponential.

Being corrected by God is not punishment, and you should never fear it. The correction of God is amazing, and it does so many things for our souls that we can't manufacture anywhere else.

I moved from my repentance chair and continued the conversation with God from my truck. "Why did you pick me?" I asked Him. The question seems simple on the surface, but it got to the root of why I was so angry. Why would He hand-select me and then let me fail?

I was not afraid of failing, per se, but in the deepest parts of my heart, I was scared of being insignificant. I was afraid that I had somehow manufactured the evidence that God had chosen me and would one day find out that none of it was real.

The Holy Spirit did not respond to my question, so I kept driving. When I parked in the gym, I again attempted to speak to Him, "Why did You pick me?" Again, He didn't answer. I finished my workout and went home. That night, I told my wife, "I think I am done following God."

Of course, she was shocked. From my wife's perspective, nothing had changed. How had I gone from being good with God to *done* with Him in a few days? Another sign of spiritual warfare is that none of it will make any sense.

My wife kept trying to figure out what changed, and the lies in my mind became lies out of my mouth, which is what the enemy wants all along. He poisons your mind in order to engage you in legal contracts that allow him to poison your reality.

Remember, a legal contract in the spirit is not a signed piece of paper, but a word. When God spoke creation into existence, He didn't sign papers. He spoke words, and reality itself bent around to honor the contract of His words. We are made in God's image, and our words carry immense significance in the spiritual realm.

The enemy had lied to me, my mind had accepted it, and my words had created legal grounds for those lies to become real.

You have to be very careful, as already mentioned in this book, about the things you say. Even God Himself will honor your words because this is how He set up everything to work.

Two types of words matter in the spiritual landscape. One is the obvious, normal definition of a "word." When you say something, it becomes a word. All words have varying degrees of power based on the conviction and alignment behind them.

The more sinister type of word is the word of the heart. When you carry a belief inside of you, the thoughts of the brain orient around it. How you answer a question in your heart becomes the legal grounds for the enemy to mess with you. If you break this down to its most basic, undeniable truth, the words of the mouth all come from the words of our hearts. This is why Scripture states, "Out of the heart the mouth speaks" (Matt. 12:34; Luke 6:45).

I had created a legal testimony against God by not answering the question with the truth. Doubt, fear, and worry about the things of God are not just an unfortunate side-effect of humanity; these things are sin.

The man says to Jesus, "Forgive me for my unbelief" (Mark 9:24). He recognized something that most of us do not: that when the Creator tells you something will happen, we are actually accusing Him of falsehood through our unbelief.

It is not enough for you to ask for things. You must request and *believe* that they will be given to you. In the moment I am describing, I was in disbelief that God would come through for me. All it took was one unanswered question to open up my heart to more lies.

My wife asked me if I had talked to anybody about it, and I said no. I did not want to be talked out of my opinion. This was another sign of deception. When you are feeding off lies, you will be hesitant to seek wise counsel. My wife said she would pray for me, and we went to bed.

When I woke up the next morning, I knew it was the day of decision. I would either repent and get back in line or walk away from God. You might be thinking that does not sound healthy, and you would be correct. This was not just a randomly bad day for me. My mind was under attack, and I had let in the thing attacking me.

I went into my office and prepared for my final conversation with God. All of this was based on a simple, disingenuous question. It was a pebble that had turned into an avalanche, not unlike what happened with Adam and Eve in the garden. We don't know how long the serpent planned his mission against humanity, but we know the decision that changed everything took a single moment.

One poor response led to humanity's ultimate downfall. There is nothing in the Bible prior to the story of Eve to indicate she was in a downward spiral. She had a simple conversation that was designed to sow doubt in her mind, and the problem existed only in her head. At the point of failure, that quiet moment of hesitation, the destiny of the human race was locked up for thousands of years. Do not underestimate the significance of how you think to yourself, about yourself, or God.

RECONCILING WITH GOD

In my car again, I sat down and asked God, one more time, why He picked me. We all crave to be chosen. Yet when we are, we want to see layers of confirmation that we are not simply making it up.

This time, I was prepared for the silence. There have been times in the past when I struggled to hear from God, and usually the answer was repentance. It wasn't that God was not speaking, but something in me that was blocking my ability to hear. Repentance is like a washcloth that wipes the debris from your eyes and ears. If there is anything blocking your ability to see, repentance will clean it up and restore your vision.

I decided to give it one last shot. Why make a life-altering decision without all the data? I quickly repented, saying, "God, I'm sorry for thinking that I know better than you, and for choosing my own way over your way."

Truthfully, my heart was not even in the right place at the time. I just wanted the data. I am continually amazed at the mercy of God because He responds when He doesn't have to. As soon as I repented, a vision swept over me.

I was 9 years old, surrounded by a group of kids. I had just moved to a new city and knew no one, but I wanted to play kickball. I thought that if I could score a point, I would finally have friends. The two team captains took turns picking players to be on their team. I waited, and waited, and waited, until there was no one left but me.

The vision zoomed forward to a conversation between an 18-year-old and his first girlfriend. I didn't want to relive this, but there I was, watching it unfold. The two kids, who had already discussed marriage and children, sat in a red Nissan Pathfinder after a date night. The girl confessed that she had been cheating on the boy. He wanted to know *why* she was cheating and with whom. It was with the boy's uncle and the pastor of the church they both attended.

In that moment, the 9-year-old who felt unworthy of being picked on the kickball field became the 18-year-old who believed the same lie, now reinforced and louder: "You aren't worth being chosen."

The vision zoomed forward again to several other times in my life where I had been broken, but also protected. The vision ended, and I sat in my chair crying, confused why God had allowed me to see things that ended such a long time ago. Some of them I remember, others I had long forgotten. The kind voice of the Holy Spirit said something that changed my perspective.

"If you must know why I picked you, here it is. You were not picked when you were nine. You were not picked when you were eighteen. You were not picked when you were twenty-five, or twenty-nine, or thirty-three—and you did not walk away."

I sat there and received His words. *Finally! An answer,* I thought. *But why are you showing this to me just now?*

He responded, "You believe you were not picked because something was wrong with you, but I do not see it that way. It is not a weakness to be the last. You refuse to believe that I would pick you to be on my team, because people didn't pick you to be on theirs."

Age regression is a well-documented psychological phenomenon. Most people experience it to some degree. It occurs when a person mentally and emotionally reverts to a younger state, often in response to stress or unresolved trauma. There is a recognized therapeutic approach called Inner Child Therapy that helps individuals address and heal these early emotional wounds.

If those wounds are not healed, we can find ourselves emotionally regressing to that earlier state in moments of stress, conflict, or fear. In my case, I believe the Holy Spirit was guiding me through a kind of "inner child healing" to help release something I had unknowingly carried for years.

Whenever we are dealing with fear, the real issue is often not what we are afraid of. It is the faith, or lack thereof, that we are injecting into the situation.

FAITH IN THE WRONG THINGS

In 2007, a patient signed up for a clinical trial of a new antidepressant. He was hurt by a recent breakup and wondered if there could be a medical fix. When he first began treatment, he found the pills to be effective at relieving his symptoms and improving his mood. After the second month of treatment, a bout of depression hit, and he decided to end his life. He ate all of his remaining capsules, 29 of them, and waited to die. As soon as he swallowed the capsules, he regretted it. He changed his mind and asked his next-door neighbor to drive him to the hospital.

When the doctors examined him, he was pale, drowsy, shaking, and had critically low blood pressure. They immediately connected him to an IV to raise his blood pressure. As his condition failed to improve after a few hours, they called on one of the doctors from the clinical trial. This doctor told hospital staff that the patient had never taken the active drug. He had been assigned the placebo capsules and had overdosed on sugar pills. Physiologically, he was dying from a perception. As soon as the patient heard the news, he made a full physical recovery.[1]

Psychosomatic pain is a neurological issue in which the brain (not the body) causes symptoms. The mind can, and often does, create physical pain based on beliefs.[2] However, it goes even deeper than that. Buried in the subconscious, deep beneath the surface, is a "control mechanism" for our reality. This is a dangerous practice without a submissive heart. In fact, I would caution you to pause here and simply ask the Holy Spirit, "Should I read this right now?" Follow whatever He tells you. If you feel at peace to continue, pray this, "Lord, please guard my heart and help me see the right way to use this."

Moshe Bar, a neuroscientist at Bar-Ilan University, says, "We see what we predict, rather than what's out there."[3] God is rapidly revealing spiritual insights at a rapid pace across the earth, even as you read this. Science does not argue with God, any more than your car argues with you.

When you build something, you expect it to work the way you built it to work. Science is uncovering parts of the mind that do not make sense unless we understand Scripture. Let us examine biblical parallels for modern-day neuroscience:

- "Jesus drew near and went with them. But their eyes were kept from recognizing Him" (Luke 24:15).
- "Now faith is the substance of things hoped for, and the evidence of things not yet seen" (Hebrews 11:1).
- "As he thinketh in his heart, so is he" (Proverbs 23:7).
- "Whatever you say, if you believe, it will be done for you" (Mark 11:23).
- "To the pure, all things are pure, but to those who are corrupted, nothing is pure" (Titus 1:15).

At a recent business conference, I spoke about the different dimensions of reality. A young business owner came up afterward and asked, "If there is one chapter of the Bible that you would recommend reading to learn more about what you talked about, what would it be?" My mind immediately jumped to Colossians 3, which calls us to orient our thinking toward spiritual realities.

In Colossians, Paul draws our attention to a higher, unseen realm that ultimately shapes how we live in this one. At the intersection of this realm (earth) and the higher realm (heaven) lies human perception. Real change begins in the higher realm of heaven, and perception is the gift that connects us to it. At that crossroad, we're given a choice. One way leads to alignment and peace, the other to struggle and anxiety.

The word "think" in Colossians 3:2 is translated from the Greek word φρονέω (*phroneō*, Strong's G5426). It means to be mentally disposed towards something, not just in your intellectual mind, but with your entire orientation. It is not a passive state; "think" is an active verb that requires agency, discipline, and a rewiring of our focus. To live from heaven's reality, we must dethrone our own compulsive fixation on this realm and train our attention to rest on the higher realm.

When I hear people speaking about faith and fear, they tend to be stuck in a linear dichotomy, with fear on one side and faith on the other. They may say, "Don't be afraid; have faith."

However, psychology tells a different story. Fear is not the absence of faith, but faith pointed in the wrong direction. If you are afraid of a bad outcome that has not yet come to pass, you are placing your conviction in that negative future—a form of faith.

I would hazard that you are not afraid that the sun will not rise in the sky tomorrow. I have not yet met any healthy individual who is so stuck in fear that they will spontaneously stop being able to breathe air. Why are you not afraid of those things? Because you don't have faith in them happening, or more so, you have faith that they will *not* suddenly be taken from you. You could say these people do not have any faith in that situation happening. Whenever a person has fear of a negative situation, they must also have *faith* in that negative situation happening. Fear cannot be powered without faith; it's just faith pointed in the *wrong* direction.

We feel fear when we inject faith into anything that God did not say. When you are fearful that your bills will not be paid, it means that you are worried about something that has not happened yet, but you are feeling a lot of faith that it will.

It is not a question of whether you are experiencing fear or faith, but what you are injecting your faith in. Paul is urging us to align with the right reality. When we fix our attention on the realities of heaven, we anchor ourselves to God's promises and learn to expect their fulfillment.

Anytime we are at the intersection between the realm of earth and the realm of heaven, we will feel the effects of our decisions. When we have faith in God's promises, we will feel hope. When we have faith in the enemy's threats, we will feel fear.

Our internal alignment does not stay private. It interacts with the world around us, and to an extent, tells it what to do. This is the principle from which all New Age heretical doctrine was founded. In the rest of this chapter, we will clean it up and restore it to a Godly, submissive worldview.

NEW AGE VS. JESUS

The quantum understanding of reality is not opposed to Scripture. It is actually circling back to truths that God established at creation. This is not coincidental. As science pushes deeper into the nature of reality, it increasingly confirms what Scripture has been telling us all along: observation affects reality, intention shapes outcomes, and belief precedes results.

New Age thought places human consciousness as the ultimate arbiter of reality. Scripture, on the other hand, places Jesus as the cornerstone upon which all reality finds alignment.

The principles work in both systems because they were built into creation itself. However, only one system correctly identifies the true hierarchy of authority and will therefore last. This distinction is crucial, especially for Christians who wonder why New Age practices sometimes seem to "work" even when they are disconnected from Jesus.

Creation responds to faith, but only if faith properly aligns with God's established order will it produce lasting fruit without destructive consequences.

Neuroscientist Anil Seth, a leading researcher on consciousness, puts it well: "We don't just passively perceive the world, we actively generate it. The world we experience comes as much, if not more, from the inside out as from the outside in." Seth's work in predictive processing highlights the growing scientific consensus that the brain constructs perception based on beliefs, expectations, and intentions. This scientific insight echoes spiritual truths Scripture has long affirmed.

I have given several lectures on the topics of New Age, manifestation, and faith, which are still available on YouTube. In discussing these topics, one of the things that always confuses me is how many Christians are completely convinced that they have no power at all. This mindset often seems less about humility and more like an attempt to avoid responsibility.

In 2 Timothy 3:5, Paul describes such people: "They will maintain the outward appearance of religion but will have repudiated its power." He warns us to "avoid people like this."

There are some things we can only understand by exploring history, and the best place to find our spiritual history is in Scripture. Many years ago, humans were put on earth to govern and rule. We were custom-coded to have dominion over the planet. All spiritual principles recognize this design.

Of course, we know that the human race fell, and for many thousands of years, creation was forced to endure a government it was never designed to endure.

Jesus later enters history to redeem the treason committed on behalf of Adam and Eve. The term "gospel" (Greek: εὐαγγέλιον, *euangelion*) was originally a political term before it became associated with religious contexts. An inscription from the year 9 B.C. known as the Priene Calendar Inscription reads, "The birthday of the god Augustus was the beginning of the good news (*euangelion*) for the world that came by reason of him."

In the Roman context, the word *eungelion* referred to official announcements of imperial victories, accession to power, or divine honors given to the emperor. When the apostles used this same word to describe Jesus, they were making a bold political and theological statement: that Jesus is the true King, inaugurating a new Kingdom. Therefore, all subjects who belonged to this new Emperor received a "reinstatement" as part of the Kingdom of God.

Creation never "forgot" what it was designed to do. It was created with rules, processes, and governance protocols. Creation did not betray man. Man betrayed creation. However, when the reinstatement happened, the original protocols were reactivated.

> *For the creation eagerly waits with anticipation for God's sons to be revealed. For the creation was subjected to futility—not willingly, but because of Him who subjected it—in the hope that the creation itself will also be set free from the bondage of corruption into the glorious freedom of God's children. For we know that the whole creation has been groaning together with labor pains until now."*
> —Romans 8:19–22 (HCSB)

First, creation was *eagerly waiting*. Creation did not enjoy the time between the fall of Adam and the death and resurrection of Jesus. It was penalized unwillingly. Second, Paul said creation was waiting for the revealing of the "sons of God." Every time this phrase is used in the time period between Adam and Jesus, it speaks of angelic beings. Every time the phrase is used in the New Testament, it refers to you and me. In other words, "We lost it because of Adam. And we have been restored to it, through Jesus."

Lastly, Paul writes, "The whole creation has been groaning together until now" (Romans 8:22). Restoration, reinstatement, and redemption are *now*, not tomorrow. Reality was structured to work a certain way, but it was corrupted. Like a computer system infected with a virus, creation knew something was wrong but could not fix itself. Jesus cleans the system and restores it to its original form and function.

When people ask me about New Age, I tell them that Romans 8:19–22 is why New Age works. Something can work in the interim and be devastating in the long term. The car would respond, not because she's qualified to drive, but because it was programmed to recognize the key. However, that situation will not end well for my daughter, who, at her current age, does not have the intelligence or the understanding to drive a car.

In the same way, creation is programmed to respond to faith, but only those aligned with God's authority are equipped to wield it well. This is why the New Age movement can tap into real spiritual principles, yet still lead people away from the truth.

When you expect something, it changes the energetic frequency around you. Part of why the Bible repeats, "Do not be afraid," is because fear itself, as we have discussed, is the key of faith just turned in the wrong direction. When we are afraid of something, we are turning a key and telling that program to bring us what we are afraid of. Creation (for example, the Tesla) will respond to its programming, whether we know how to use it or not.

Why did Jesus often caveat His promises about prayer by saying, "If you believe it will happen"? That is because faith is the key. God responds to your faith, but so does creation. James seconds this: "But let him ask in faith without doubting. For the doubter is like the surging sea, driven and tossed by the wind" (James 1:6). The doubter is confusing the programmed response of creation itself. Instead of offering a steady directive, they transmit instability, uncertainty, and contradiction.

When my child asks me for something, I am usually excited to help them get it. I can tell when one of my kids is trying to manipulate me into getting something they shouldn't have, or whether they're just hungry and need something to eat. That is the same way Jesus tells us how we should approach God as Father when we're in need of something. In Luke 11:11, he says, "Are any of you fathers? What kind of father would give his son a snake when he asks for food? Or if your son asked for dinner, would you give him a scorpion? No father would actually do that."

> *"So if sinful people know how to give good gifts to their children, how much more will your heavenly Father give the Holy Spirit to those who ask him."*
> —*Luke 11:13 (NLT)*

One of my favorite things to do is to show people how much God cares about them. Contrary to popular belief, He does not get offended when you ask Him for things. However, there are rules for how the program has been set up.

We see many times in Scripture where God honored His word and His structure. Even when someone might have needed a solution, they did not get it because they abandoned the process. One of the most essential structures we have to learn is to operate in the structure of faith.

Fear is a corruption of the faith structure, and it always comes as a result of the one tool the enemy knows how to use: doubt. From the very beginning of the Bible when he approached Eve, until the present moment, the enemy has had but one tool. If he can get you to doubt yourself, doubt your Father, or place your faith in worst-case scenarios, he will successfully sabotage you.

The enemy has not been permitted to touch you in the natural, unless you give him permission to do so. You are, after all, a ruler in this realm. He will, however, take whatever privileges you willingly give him.

When we learn to stand on promises and speak those promises, we build up faith within ourselves for the things God has spoken. Again, faith comes by *hearing*, and hearing by the word of God. It is important to memorize and successfully speak the words of God over yourself and over your life.

When we do not, we will not have the answers to the questions that come through the serpent. An unanswered or poorly answered question gives the enemy a permission slip to affect you in ways you do not want.

THE ALTAR OF GENEROSITY

"There is one who scatters, yet increases more; and there is one who withholds more than is right, but it leads to poverty."
—Proverbs 11:24–25

In classical, Newtonian mechanics, a cause leads to an effect like clockwork. You push the ball, and it rolls. As Newton stated in his First Law of Motion, "An object at rest stays at rest, and an object in motion stays in motion, unless acted upon by an external force." However, in the early 20th century, experiments began revealing phenomena that did not fit this deterministic view, starting with Max Planck's work on blackbody radiation. This marked the birth of quantum mechanics, which challenged classical assumptions.

What happens when what you believed to be the absolute truth turns out to be fundamentally uncertain? Many of the pioneering scientists of the early 20th century faced this reality.

The philosophical foundations that had supported their understanding of the universe were shaken, and they had to wrestle with God and science in ways they were unprepared to do.

Wolfgang Pauli, a brilliant theoretical physicist, suffered his first mental breakdown in the 1930s. Albert Einstein kept changing his mind every few years about just about everything. For the first time in modern science, these Newtonian scientists found themselves grappling with existential questions, embracing a philosophy centered on human agency and the role of consciousness in shaping reality.

Newtonian science was all about the physics of things: the right thing, in the right order, producing consistently "right" results. Quantum mechanics was changing the order of causation and replacing external phenomena with internal phenomena. For example, in Newtonian science, we would say that to get a light to turn on, you must flip the switch on. In the quantum world, there is an additional step that can sometimes eliminate the need to flip the switch in the first place.

The added step exists *before* the activity occurs, and it starts with your mind, thoughts, attention, and expectations. An array of possibilities is "superimposed" into a cosmic ocean of distinct outcomes. We can categorically sum up the control mechanism used to select these outcomes individually and bring them into reality with what's loosely called your "state." Your state comprises your mind, your thoughts, your attention, and your expectations. To turn a light on, you must get "in state," which allows you to flip the switch first.

In Newtonian logic, reality is controlled by actions that trigger a response. In quantum logic, reality waits. It holds a series of possibilities suspended in time, waiting to identify your intention. Once it identifies your intention, it condenses (or collapses) all available outcomes into one outcome (the end result).

Uncertainty, then, is a feature, not a bug. It can also be profound and opportunistic. Humans tend to eliminate uncertainty, thinking they are creating something predictable and logical. However, it is in this zone of uncertainty that God causes promotion to occur. God is, after all, the one who set all this up.

Humans didn't "invent" mathematics; we discovered it. It worked long before we were aware of it. Similarly, we did not "invent" the realm of energy; we merely discovered that it was already set up many years ago in an intelligent, orderly fashion.

When Isaac Newton began publishing his research, it infiltrated everything, including medicine, psychology, mathematics, physics, and even spirituality to an extent. Before Newton, the church and science were linked together.[1] The first "scientists," by basic definition, were the ancient spiritual leaders (including the Hebrews) trying to understand *why* things happened.[2] Almost all cultures, from the ancient Babylonians and Egyptians to the Chinese philosophers, have designed sophisticated astronomical and mathematical knowledge banks.

After the 18th century, things began to separate. The "Enlightenment" began to promote reason and rationalism over spirituality and revelation. A closer look reveals that this division was driven by power dynamics. Scientists, who were almost all spiritually inclined like Newton, wanted to discover the beauty of God's creation. The church wanted to maintain its dominance. That led to the separation of the scientific from the spiritual disciplines.

Before this, as in the time of Jesus, they were almost inextricably linked together. As Jesus said, "You are like a seed. Unless you fall to the ground and die, you can't grow" (John 12:24). This explains the scientific process of how a tree becomes planted and tended. Likewise, a caterpillar must experience a death of sorts for the butterfly to emerge.

However, the separation between science and spirituality went too far. What Newton designed for governing physics was taken and extrapolated throughout culture. The four central tenets of Newtonian science were applied to mainstream thinking, and we lost our eye for the supernatural. People began to filter everything through the lens of determinism, reductionism, objectivity, and materialism.

- **Determinism:** If you know the present, you can predict the future.
- **Reductionism:** Understand the whole by dissecting the parts.
- **Objectivity:** The observer is separate from the observed.
- **Materialism:** Only physical matter is real.

One of the most brilliant scientific minds in history, Lord Kelvin, famously said, "There is nothing new to be discovered in physics now. All that remains is more and more precise measurement."[3] However, five years later, Albert Einstein published his theory of relativity. Within twenty-five years, the quantum theory emerged, and we discovered that even minds like Lord Kelvin's can be brilliantly *incorrect* due to limited perspective.

In the 1970s, David Bohm presented his implicit versus explicit order findings. As it turns out, the observer is not separate from the observed, and everything is connected. As it turns out, physical matter is the least real thing in our universe. Everything is created first in nonphysical reality.

We had previously known this, but humans like to eventually control things. You can see this illustrated beautifully in Plato's famous "Allegory of the Cave," written in 380 B.C. Plato describes a prisoner chained in a cave since birth, facing a blank wall. Behind him, a fire cast shadows on the wall from objects passing between the fire and the prisoner. Because the shadows were all he had ever seen, the prisoner believed they were reality.

What the prisoner saw was not reality itself, but a distorted projection of it. Plato's point was profound: what we perceive is often just a shadow of what's really there. Even thousands of years ago, we understood that the surface of things is rarely the whole story.

In recent years, a reintegration has begun taking place. People are beginning to pay attention to spirituality as a causal piece of the overall "shadow" of reality. In the 1980s, Werner Erhard began to teach the masses about this structure of reality. He taught a formula for achievement that started with "being."

If you have ever seen the framework BE > DO > HAVE, you have seen Erhard's teaching. Most modern coaches, from Tony Robbins to Bob Proctor, have taught some variation of this model. And where does the model come from? Ancient Scripture.

Here is how the BE > DO > HAVE framework aligns with biblical principles:

> "Let us make man in our image…" (BE)
> "Let them rule…" (DO)
> "They will be fruitful…" (HAVE)[4]

From Ephesians 2:10, we read, "We are His workmanship (BE), created in Christ Jesus to do good works (DO), which God prepared in advance for us to walk in (HAVE)" (Ephesians 2:10). Again, in John 15:5, we have, "I am the vine; you are the branches. If you abide in me (BE), you will bear much fruit (DO)… this is to my Father's glory, that you will bear much fruit (HAVE)" (John 15:5).

God always begins by establishing an identity. He gives a name, a purpose, and an organizational infrastructure to govern our existence. He then instructs us on how we are to behave, and then He multiplies everything around us.

Now, how does any of this integrate with finance, currency, and wealth? We must begin to look at the spiritual world with a fresh vision. It is not enough to understand altars and idols. We must replace false systems with true ones.

GENEROSITY AS CAUSE, NOT EFFECT

The Bible is more than a historical text. It includes instructions on how we were built to operate. It also teaches us how the spiritual world works and how we are meant to participate in it.

Generosity is one such key that activates systems in the spiritual realm. Repentance is another key. Forgiveness is still another. All throughout Scripture, we find keys. I call them keys because they are more than guidelines. Generosity, for instance, creates expansion faster than almost anything else.

As you shift the way you think and view the world, reality shifts with you. This is not New Age; this is the Bible. All New Age thinking has done is copy pieces and parts of the Way: the manuscript of the ages, also known as Scripture or God's Word.

We live within an information field, or a spiritual and energetic structure that records everything that exists. Thankfully, we are not left to navigate this on our own. God has given us the roadmap, and obedience to this roadmap will create progress in many areas of your life, not just financial.

Humans were not built to exist in one dimension. We were designed to exist in multiple planes and realities at the same time, natural and spiritual, seen and unseen.

Over time, Satan has weaponized ignorance against the church and believers. Throughout Scripture, you hear God repeat that his people were being destroyed for lack of knowledge. We were not made to forget, and we were not designed to die. Death was brought about as the cost of disobedience.

Our minds and bodies were created to govern and rule over creation. Yet, because we have forgotten how, we struggle to keep up. We pollute our inner "software" with sin, doubt, and ignorance. A good part of this book has been an honest admission of how many times I have known something about God, and yet not trusted Him to care for me. That is called doubt. As James wrote in Scripture, doubt causes you to be tossed around on the waves of fate (see James 1:6). It eliminates the key needed to govern and enforce God's will effectively through prayer. Without faith and trust, our connection to God's power is weakened.

This principle applies not only to prayer but also to how generosity functions in the spiritual realm. It is important to understand how generosity powers expansion. If we were to define electrical energy, we might say energy is a flow, or potential flow, of charge between a high-energy area and a low-energy area.[5]

Any surface area that is latent is usually a high-energy area. If you took a ball and held it in the air over your head, it would technically be a high-energy object, because the *potential* energy in the ball is maxed out. It has the capacity and the potential to create movement. As soon as you let the ball go, gravity will kick in, and the ball will begin to expend energy by falling.

One way to look at the power of energy is to define its potential. Something is high-energy if there is a lot of potential force waiting to be released. If the energy is converted into reality, it would have a lot of force. Therefore, a bowling ball would have more energy than a tennis ball. However, this energy is not lost when it is converted. It is merely transformed and transferred to something else, then ripples out.

Our bodies operate according to these same principles. Nerve cells use electrical currents to generate and transfer energy. Inside a fully charged nerve cell, there is a higher concentration of potassium ions on the inside and sodium ions on the outside. The difference in charge between the inside and outside of the cell represents stored energy. It functions like a battery with a positive charge on one side and a negative charge on the other. When a nerve signal is fired, sodium ions rush into the cell. This sudden influx of positive charges creates an electrical spike that travels down the nerve cell like a wave.

Afterward, the cell must reset. This reset process uses an energy-dependent pump to push sodium ions back out of the cell and pull potassium ions back in. Once the reset is complete, the cell is recharged and ready, holding potential energy once again.

Notice that when the cell is full of sodium, it cannot fire correctly. The sodium must be pushed out and put back on the outside, requiring the use of insulin.

Consider a person with diabetes who is unable to utilize insulin to activate the reset function of a cell's battery. When a person's life lacks generosity, they are experiencing a form of spiritual diabetes. They can be surrounded by energy (abundance) and unable to access it. Without generosity, there is no activation of spiritual transference. The "cell" never resets. The system breaks down. Over time, this damages a person's financial health, relational health, and even their ability to receive.

When a person lacks generosity, they stagnate, experience blockages, and their production capacity is damaged. The ancient Hebrews called this *tzedakah*, or "charity." However, the root meaning is righteousness. Generosity is one of the ways we fundamentally align with the will of God in righteousness.

When Jesus talked about generosity, he added layers of meaning. Recall the story of the poor woman who gave less than everyone else, though it was all she had. The costly nature imbued into her giving was more potent than the larger offerings others made, but without having to make a relative sacrifice.

Like an electrical signal, triggering a wave over the cell of a body, the woman's generosity sent out a massive wave capable of triggering a yield from the world around her. When you combine science and spirituality, you get more than just a recommendation. Spiritual law works like gravity. You either obey it or you don't.

Most people chase "more" because they are afraid of the future. Their attention is trapped in a short-term cycle of fear, production, and worry. These are the consequences of following mammon. It is the voice that says, "No one is coming to save you. You have to save yourself." However, Biblical instruction counteracts that idea.

When you hoard and manipulate, you shrink. When you give and trust, you expand. The quantum world punishes anything with fear attached to it. You get to decide whether you want to work uphill and against the grain, or whether you want to flow with the designed order and work inside of God's way.

"There is one who gives freely," Proverbs 11:24 says, "yet grows all the richer; another withholds what he should give, and only suffers want." This is true because giving and receiving are both a transference of energy. One goes out, the other comes in.

Your intangible life is a series of gates. These gates are either opened or closed based on what you believe and what you do. What you have is a result of what is coming through these gates. Notice, this follows the same structure: Be, Do, Have. What you believe is who you are, or the organizing principle of identity. Who you are determines what you do. And what you do determines what you have.

When we build generous lives, we open the gates of our lives to receive financial increase. When we withhold out of fear, we close the gates required to be open for our ultimate expansion.

GRATITUDE

To successfully understand the systems God built into the fabric of the universe, we have to understand the cause-and-effect relationships between things. Manifestation, for instance, is nothing more than expectation and intention. The problem with "New Age" manifestation is that it feeds the altar of Baal, which erases the proper hierarchy. We are not at the top. Jesus is, and anything we do apart from Jesus will fail in the long run.

Jesus told us this in John 15:5, "Apart from me, you can do nothing." That is a pretty basic, self-explanatory law. The universe itself is built upon God's laws and His words. When we read verses about faith, we see where the New Age practitioners got many of their ideas. Many popular New Age proponents will say, "Oh, well, the Bible was not the first place this was all written. The Bible technically copied the laws of hermetics." This isn't true. They just don't know where hermetics came from.

Hermeticism is thought to have come from Hermes, the mythical syncretic figure based on a blend of Greek and Egyptian mythology. However, way before this, we had two humans, one male and one female, who were placed in a garden and charged with stewarding the information of heaven to govern the Earth.

In their journey, they sinned more than once. The first sin committed was not just disobedience, but also doubt. Without doubt, Eve never would have disobeyed the words of God. If Adam was present at the beginning and received the divine instruction God gave him before the Fall, he would have passed this information along to his children. However, sin occurred again. Cain, the son who killed his brother, ran away and founded a city. Things quickly got much worse.

According to the Bible, this led to a time of great evil to plague the earth. Divine figures rebelled and began teaching forbidden knowledge, such as astrology, seduction, and divination. Adam would have known about these things already, not because God gave him a secret download, but because he was with these divine figures when he was in charge of the Earth. The fallen angels would have known exactly who Adam was, as Adam's position outranked many of them.

Now, if I wanted to secure a meeting with a king or a president or someone else very important, I likely could not just walk up and talk to them. If I can even secure a meeting at all, it would be with many protections in place. Adam was high enough in the hierarchy of the Earth that Satan could not approach him directly without deception. He had to appear as a serpent, an animal that Adam likely named and had dominion over. It was a covert operation, like a spy infiltrating a presidential cabinet.

That breach, which was subtle at first, widened over generations. The knowledge once protected by God's order eventually fell into the hands of those who would use it to build entire systems of rebellion.

These "secrets" consolidated around a powerful figure in history known as Nimrod. He used them to build a gate to the supernatural, known in our Bibles as the Tower of Babel. From here, the knowledge was scattered, and history created many more branches. From these branches come almost all of the religions of the world, including the secret mystery schools that turned into Gnosticism. They all take parts of the truth and twist it to fit a narrative of self-advancement, control, and manipulation.

LOOKING FOR JESUS

I have spoken at business conferences and meetups all over the world, and I can tell you with certainty that everyone is looking for Jesus. They just do not know that "Jesus" is His name.

People look for Jesus in psychedelics, New Age, money, sex, movies, businesses, and all kinds of crazy places. They might feel a glimpse of peace, a flash of truth, and a sense for the first time in their lives that everything really could be okay. Then, at the end of that pursuit, they learn that what they were feeling was not just temporary inspiration. It is a Person, and He has a name.

If you could design the perfect God for yourself, what features would you give him? He would be kind. He would forgive you, because we all do things wrong sometimes. He would be powerful and protect you from things that you cannot defend yourself from. He would be able to see the future, and maybe even change things in your past, too. He would smile, embrace you, and tell you what to do when you cannot figure it out on your own. He would never force you into things but instead invite you to participate.

Everyone would unwittingly design Jesus. Yet he already exists, and one of my favorite things in the world is watching people realize that. Recently, I stood in front of a room full of people and took them through a form of spiritual "inner child therapy," and watched them experience a sweep of emotions. Everyone was crying. Then they were laughing and feeling inspired and empowered. Some of them were hearing for the first time ever that everything was going to be okay. That is what Jesus does.

Yet instead of introducing people to Him, many Christians run for the hills anytime something even remotely *sounds* like New Age or Eastern spirituality. Meanwhile, New Age seekers are some of our most engaged online audiences. Many are already trying to find their way to the next level. Imagine their surprise when the very thing they have been searching for is right in front of them, and it's Jesus.

It is not true that we are living in the most evil times. There are plenty of times before us when evil operated in the open, and the earth was ruled through the occult. From the days before the flood, the primary inclination of the human heart was persistent evil (Genesis 6:5). Entire civilizations were built on the worship of false gods and the practices of divination, sorcery, and child sacrifice. In many ways, today's rebellion is more covert, but no less real. New Age, Gnosticism, and the mystery schools are not new ideas. They are old systems rooted in half-truths, distorted wisdom, and spiritual shortcuts.

This is why it's so important to understand the nature of deception. There is only one Truth, but the lie isn't always the obvious opposite. No one chooses a blatant falsehood when given the full truth. The most dangerous lies are half-truths, twisted just enough to keep people confused and wandering.

We must stop running from what we do not understand and learn how to talk to Jesus about everything. One of the more profound byproducts of having the right spiritual systems in place and truly communing with God is gratitude.

Gratitude is a spiritual tool that enforces God's will in a person. Philippians 4:6 says, "Don't be pulled in different directions or worried about a thing. Be saturated in prayer throughout each day, offering your faith-filled requests before

God with overflowing gratitude. Tell Him every detail of your life."

Gratitude is a key to activating faith. Whenever you feel a lack of faith, gratitude is one of the most powerful ways to get back in alignment. There is a growing body of peer-reviewed research confirming that gratitude enhances productivity, decision-making, mental resilience, and even financial health. But the Bible already told us this.

One of my favorite studies comes from Charles Schwab & Co., where a leader implemented a gratitude practice using index cards to document employee contributions. She would share these observations through emails, audio messages, and meetings. Within one year, her division jumped from the second-lowest to the second-highest in employee engagement across the company.

Read the Word of God. And then do what it says. When you re-align with God's promises, which are found in Scripture, you will begin to see your life differently. You will begin to see yourself differently, and the overflow that follows will be profound.

GODLY INCREASE

"The blessing of the Lord makes a person rich, and he adds no sorrow to it."
—*Proverbs 10:22*

It should be obvious that God intended for us to live in abundance. Yet you can know something to be true but not know how to use it. Believing God can do something is quite different than believing God can do it through or for you. Imagine how David felt after being anointed, before becoming king. He was uncelebrated. He was unknown and underrated, and the people who did know him still thought of him as a child.

The first king in Israel's history was celebrated and cherished. Yet David, the future king of Israel, was abandoned as an outcast. The Bible is full of stories like this. It's clear that God has a special interest in hidden and overlooked people.

However, being chosen by God does not mean being instantly elevated, and this tension between promise and process can be one of the greatest tests of faith. That is the problem we must overcome in our belief systems. And then we must partner with God by submitting to His timelines and His principles of His will.

THE HOMELESS MAN IN MY OFFICE

A few years ago, I was hosting an event. Conferences like this are recorded to be shared with clients or attendees, so there is always a crew in the back handling cameras and sound.

During one of the breaks, a guy running a camera called me over. I had never seen him before. He started talking about how the Bible validated everything I was saying from the stage. Everything this person said was packed with so much understanding and revelation that it took me a while to process.. I was overwhelmed by his knowledge and surprised that a random cameraman was running laps around me in his understanding of the Bible. I remember thinking, *This guy is smarter than anyone I've ever had running cameras.* We talked for a few more minutes before I had to move on to the next session.

I did not connect with him again until 2024, when he showed up at my house to interview for one of our (then) new brands, The Deep End. The Deep End was maybe two months old at this point, and my producer, Jake, recommended we get this guy on to interview him. Sure enough, he put on a masterclass of history combined with theology in a way I'd never seen before.

After the interview, I asked him what he was doing with his life. He told me he no longer runs cameras at my events. He had just finished a book and was preparing to start an organization to help people with spiritual deliverance. He was working a lot but sleeping on a couch at his friend's house.

My specialty since 2015 has been helping businesses scale through teams, online media, advertising, and product development. We have several brands now that branch out into spirituality, psychology, and media, but the main throughput and cash cow business has always been helping companies grow. I know how to build financial resources quickly. When I was about to start offering him advice on how to build his organization, it felt like I was stepping into a familiar rhythm. However, the Holy Spirit gave me a clear picture of a waterfall of resources pouring toward him.

So I shifted gears and asked him if he was ready to handle a lot of money. He shook it off and said something like, "I don't care about that."

"You might not, but God cares a lot about it," I said. "I'm telling you that you would be walking into some major financial increase. Call me when you need me." That was the end of the conversation, but not our friendship.

Since then, this man has gotten married and is no longer homeless. He vacations in Italy with his family, and people randomly send him thousands of dollars at a time. His business and team are growing exponentially. He is giving away close to half of his income, but it just keeps growing anyway.

But the increase does not come without struggle. He called me a few months ago and told me, "The Promised Land is almost harder than the desert."

When you think money will solve all your problems, it can be shocking to find out that it does not. No amount of money can fix a broken life or a broken identity.. If your life is truly broken, no amount of money can fix it.

I have seen business owners get wildly rich and then lose their families because they could not carry the weight of money. I have seen people die from heart attacks and stress related to the toil they put into increasing their position. The altar of Baal, the relentless pursuit of more, does not bring life, only destruction.

Now, what if you are in a position where you fully trust God, but just do not know how to position yourself correctly? We will finish this book with some practical instructions on how to prepare yourself for Godly increase.

God gives us all the principles. We just need to follow them. All throughout the Bible, there are instructions that can be hard to follow but always pay off.

- Whoever is kind to the poor lends to the Lord. Proverbs 19:17 (NIV)
- If you spend yourselves on behalf of the hungry and satisfy the needs of the oppressed, then your light will rise in the darkness. Isaiah 58:10 (NIV)
- Blessed is the one who considers the poor! In the day of trouble, the Lord delivers him. Psalm 41:1 (NIV)
- The generous will themselves be blessed, for they share their food with the poor. Proverbs 22:9 (NIV)
- If anyone has material possessions and sees a brother or sister in need but has no pity on them, how can the love of God be in that person? 1 John 3:17 (NIV)

God is very interested in equipping people with resources, but not without requirements and context. The blessing of the Lord is not for the purposes of hoarding and accumulation. It is to help the people who do not have what they need. This does not mean you cannot have a lavish lifestyle, only that you cannot live your life thinking only about yourself.

Whenever I say this publicly on a platform like our YouTube channel, I inevitably get comments along the lines of, *"Easy for you to say, you are rich."* However, those people do not know my story. They don't know that for years, we had nothing. That we were living paycheck to paycheck, just like them. What they *really* don't know is how my wife gave to others, even when we barely had anything to offer. One time, at a church service, my wife was so moved by compassion for an individual that we gave them everything we had in our bank account. That person did not know it was all we had. (And I didn't know either. I found out later, and I'll be honest, I was not happy.)

The ultimate test of godliness is how you behave when you do not have much. Money only multiplies your idols. If you are greedy when you lack resources, you will be even greedier when you have them. If you are afraid when you lack resources, you will be more afraid when you have them. Money simply multiplies what's already there.

If we are going to talk about managing or multiplying money, we must understand where it came from. The invention of monetary policy and currency allowed the human race to specialize. Specialization allows one person to go really deep into a certain industry or topic and get really good at it. They can only do that because they don't have to be great at everything. Medicine, music, and science have all advanced significantly because of specialization. Understanding this system, even on a cursory level, is crucial for learning how to manage money effectively.

THE SHOEMAKER BUSINESS

Imagine you are a professional shoemaker living several thousand years ago in a little village. You are the only shoemaker for hundreds of miles. You don't even have to be that good at making shoes. If nobody else is around to make shoes, you have a chokehold on the shoe business in your area. Demand is steady, but your supply is limited.

In money systems today, we have "supply and demand" curves, which are the basis for how expensive something is. Everybody needs shoes (demand), and only you can make them (supply). This is good for you, and it means you can charge whatever you want. The fewer shoes you make, the more expensive they become.

In some markets today, we have "secondary" markets where there is a second supply-and-demand curve. Some industries use these secondary markets to help stabilize the primary market. For example, the brand Rolex only offers its pieces to authorized dealers. You cannot buy a Rolex directly from the brand. This creates two markets: the primary market is the Rolex product sold to the authorized dealers, and the secondary market is where individual customers buy the product from the authorized dealers. This allows Rolex to control the supply-and-demand ratio based on the economy and the demand for its products. Oil is another market that uses secondary markets as a tool for price stabilization.

As a shoemaker in that time period, money as a currency did not exist yet, so there was no standard value attached to any type of currency. You had to sell the shoes you made through bartering. People would trade whatever they were good at making to get the thing you were good at making. A trade might have included livestock, food, clothing, or spices in exchange for your shoes.

Now, here is the problem. Not everybody agreed on how much things are worth. Value is highly subjective and purely based on need. If crops had a bad season, nobody would trade their food for a pair of shoes. On the other hand, if the harvest was especially rich, someone might have been happy to trade several bushels of whatever food they grew for a pair of decent shoes.

All great currencies have the following things in common:

- Agreed-upon value.
- They are traceable, meaning you have to be able to track them through a ledger or a record-keeping system.
- They can be owned.
- They are stable.
- They are fractal, so you can divide the currency into smaller units.

Bartering is very different from purchasing within a currency-based monetary system. Let's say your business is doing well, and your product is in demand. You look for a builder who can build you a house. A builder isn't going to trade a house for a pair of shoes. You might need to barter two hundred pairs of shoes for the house, but this person does not need shoes from you.

What you would have to do, if you didn't want to build the house yourself, is find everything else this person wanted or needed and trade your shoes for those things. That would make you a broker or market maker, someone who mediates or oversees transactions for end users.

The problem with barter economics is that you can't just be a shoemaker. You've got to become a part-time merchant and then broker every single time you need something. The builder wants food for his family. He wants clothes. He wants spices or rare jewels to give to his wife. Your job would have to be to go find all of those things, trade your shoes for them, and then store them to give to your builder. Not all at once, by the way, because payment is never given up front, but in stages. It's enormously complicated and would have required way too much attention.

When you think about the constraint this would have placed on your ability to produce shoes, it would be tyrannical and absurd. And this is why specialization, real mastery of a craft, couldn't emerge until currency was developed. Nobody could afford to get good at any one thing because they spent half their time trading just to survive.

But there's another problem here that's even more worrisome: price elasticity. The entire system was fundamentally unstable at its core.

Let's say another shoemaker moves into town; now you've got competition. When there are too many shoes, the value goes down. A year ago, you could have brokered two hundred pairs of shoes for a house. The exchange rate would have required two hundred shoes to equal the value of a fully built house. But if there are too many shoes for any given market, what happens to the value of each individual pair of shoes? It goes down.

The market is now saturated with shoes. Nobody needs more shoes. Because of the supply and demand equation, you now need four hundred pairs of shoes to equal the value of a fully built house, not two hundred. You've got to work twice as hard, produce twice as much, run around town twice as long, and for what? The same outcome you would have been able to get a year ago for half the effort.

A sophisticated civilization cannot function this way. We invented currency as a way to help provide fair and stable market value for goods and services. But we haven't fixed all of it. We have these incredible technological innovations in currency: digital payments, cryptocurrency, instant transfers, and the greatest current feat of engineering in modern currency, the US dollar. Yet there are still areas of the economy operating on ancient bartering systems.

A few years ago, I sat down with one of our real estate financial controllers to look over an international deal I was considering. The location was on the beaches of the Dominican Republic. The controller explained to me that the maintenance crews who would be doing the renovations on the deal did not want money. They wanted to be paid in cigars.

She explained that the owner of the crew had been doing this for a while and could make more money selling the cigars than he could by taking cash. The exchange rate was poor, and the cigars offered better value.

THE OLDEST CURRENCY IN THE WORLD

The oldest recorded "currency" in the world was the rai stone. Rai stones, which were valued based on size, were one of humankind's first attempts to attach value to something that wasn't the thing they were selling or buying.

The rai stone was a disc-shaped rock with holes drilled in it. The smallest stones could be an inch in diameter, and some of the largest ones weighed over 800 pounds. Although they were not fractal or divisible, they could at least be differentiated by size.

If you had been a shoemaker in those times, you would have tried to trade your shoes for small rai stones. After you collected, let's say, a dozen rai stones, you could trade them in for a bigger one. When a rai stone was traded, a transaction was scratched onto the surface with the new owner, noting a change in ownership.

There were two major problems with this system, however. One was that you cannot move large rai stones very well. The second was that anyone could scratch out a name and put themselves as the owner. This prevented communities from trading with the outside world.

MODERN CURRENCY

Currently, the United States' central banking system, the Federal Reserve, has managed to keep our currency system afloat for several years. That does not mean the system is without its problems. It simply means that it is stable enough to support trade systems and for people to continue in specialization.

Inflation is a real thing, and if you have been paying attention, you have probably seen the headlines about it over the last few years. Every global superpower that has successfully moved a currency away from inherent value backing has fallen. The checks and balances of supply-and-demand mechanisms have, thus far, kept the United States from experiencing similar declines.

Many formidable thinkers believe we are on the edge of a global restructuring due to the complex nuances in trade, production, and currency. The main problem with our currency, and the aspect we will talk about in the rest of this chapter, is the supply aspect of the supply-and-demand curve.

Essentially, if you want a currency to be stable and sustainable, you must make it hard to produce. If something is easy to create, supply could simply outpace demand, and that is a recipe for inflation.

Inflation is simply what happens when the buying power of a currency declines. When we used gold as a currency, the only way to increase the supply was to mine it. Historically, the global supply of gold has grown from 1.5 percent to 2 percent annually. That built-in scarcity kept inflation in check.

During the COVID-19 pandemic, the Federal Reserve added an additional 28 percent to the money supply, far more than 1.5 percent. When this happens, purchasing power goes down. This is why the average cost of a home in 1920 was between $4,000 and $6,000, while the average cost of a home in 2025 is around $400,000. There was suddenly a lot more money, but the production (which is required for demand) did not increase in direct proportion.

A hundred years ago, you could store money in a safe deposit box, and the value would increase. Now, if you saved money in a bank, the value decreases by a few percentage points a year. It makes almost zero sense to save all of your money, because the most purchasing power you will ever get out of that money is right now. We can tie the growing wealth gap (the discrepancy between the rich and the poor) to this as well.

The increasing return on capital is outpacing the return on labor. That means you can never "get ahead" by working more or working harder. It isn't just difficult; it's mathematically impossible.

The only way to get ahead is by drastically increasing your value proposition to the world. That involves thinking creatively to solve problems, because people will always pay a premium for others to solve their problems.

The rarest asset in the world is a mind that is filled with the Holy Spirit and aware of the problems that need to be solved in the world around you. That is why one of my businesses is designed to help people build and grow creative companies that meet the needs of people around them. However, thinking outside the box requires you to think differently and "upgrade" parts of your brain that might be on autopilot. Thankfully, Scripture gives us clear, practical clues for becoming financially free.

SPIRITUAL PRINCIPLES FOR INCREASE

One of the best lessons in financial management from Scripture is the ability to steward the money we already have. I have a good friend who writes music in Nashville. She and her husband make decent money, and they prayed to God for wisdom on what to do with it. This couple often buys the most random houses in unknown, obscure areas.

One time, I asked why she bought a house in a city where nobody else was investing in that I knew of. She said, "God told me to," and that was the end of it. A few years later, that city was busting at the seams; everyone was escaping the central city to move into this suburb, which created a massive multiple on the couple's investment.

In Psalm 24:1 (NIV), we read, "The earth and everything in it, the world and its inhabitants, belong to the LORD." It might be a good idea to begin asking God what to do with what you already have. He knows where the assets he's given you are going to go, and He can give you a unique direction to bless you.

Another principle from Scripture instructs us to use our gifts to serve people and solve problems. As 1 Peter 4:10 (NIV) says, every believer has received grace gifts, so use them to serve one another as faithful stewards of the many-colored tapestry of God's grace. For example, if you have a speaking gift, do it as though God were speaking his words through you. If you have the gift of serving, do it passionately with the strength God gives you, so that in everything, God alone will be glorified through Jesus Christ.

God has given me unique talents that I am using to spread His messages, and in return, He is using them to bless me financially. You will never solve big problems without the opportunity to have God bless you financially. In fact, the bigger the problem you are solving, the more you will get paid for the solution. Proverbs 22:29 tells us that mastery is a pathway to promotion: If you are uniquely gifted in your work, you will rise and be promoted. You won't be held back; you'll stand before kings!

Time preference and delayed gratification are other principles from Scripture that are designed to empower us to be financially and spiritually blessed (see Proverbs 21:5 [NIV]). Even investment principles can be found in Scripture. In Ecclesiastes 11:2 (NIV), we read: "Divide your investments among many places, for you do not know what risks might lie ahead."

In Exodus 18:17–21, we learn that God is interested in systems and structure. He wants you to begin to notice patterns. Moses was in trouble for not paying attention to his training. He was instructed to appoint leaders and governors to manage his workload and responsibilities. Throughout the entire narrative of Scripture, we see the principle at work. God intends for you to live abundantly. In Deuteronomy 8:18 (NIV), it says explicitly that God is the one who gives you the ability to create wealth.

This is the difference between the One True God and all the counterfeits. No other deity trusts people enough to give them the choice to misuse their gift. Only Yahweh does that. If you were going to serve Baal, you had to do exactly what he told you to do, or you would be destroyed. Astarte, Ashtoreth, Ishtar, and Molech all promised riches, power, and influence, but ruled through fear, manipulation, and strict conditions, not freedom.

Only Yahweh gave gifts to His people and trusted them. Whenever I look at people who do not know God but are prospering anyway, I think about this. They were given the ability by God to create wealth. That is a facet of God's personality. He alone, among all the other gods who jostle for posture and position, was confident enough to give the gift first, then let us decide what to do with it.

In an astounding play of trust and kindness, Yahweh allows us to use His gifts, knowing full well that we might not always turn back to Him with the byproduct. My encouragement to you as we end this book is simply to never forget.

Remember to always turn your heart back to the giver of all good gifts. There will never be a gift that is more valuable than the Giver.

In the end, it is all His.

NEXT STEPS

The fundamental "operating procedure" for how I approach every project in my life has crystallized in the last several years. It fits into an easy framework: "God, what do you want me to do with this? What is the play here?" This wasn't always how I operated. But I've discovered that God always has a plan. My attempts to construct alternate plans are inefficient. I'd rather skip the middle and get to the part where I know what God is doing.

In March of 2025, when I was wrestling with the final manuscript for his book, I took what you might call a strategic retreat with my wife to the mountains. I was experiencing what happens when your current competency can't solve a problem. I had written the manuscript for the book twice already, and was about to start over again. There was something just outside my grasp that I knew was essential, but I couldn't figure it out.

One evening, sitting by a fire and staring off at nothing in particular, I heard the word "Novos" pop into my brain. I had never heard of this word before, which signaled that it was outside of my existing knowledge. I thought, *Hmm... I wonder if that is something I am supposed to study.* I made a mental note to go look up the word later because I didn't have my phone with me. But God doesn't already operate in *our* timelines. He was ready to talk *right then.*

He was downloading something, and although I hadn't planned on it, I decided to keep the transmission window open. I went inside to grab a notebook and started writing. What followed was a brain dump of the last 100 years of human psychological progress. It wasn't granular enough to see exact dates, but I knew this was something God wanted me to know, and an instruction was sure to follow. This is often how the Spirit of God will speak prophetically: not as "data points," but as meaningful patterns that your spirit will recognize before your mind has a chance to categorize.

I had a deep sense that something had gone very wrong.

The reality is this: while our external world continues to improve dramatically—life expectancy is up, monetary wellbeing is improving, access to information is at an unprecedented level—*our internal systems are deteriorating at an alarming rate.* Depression rates have never been higher. PTSD and trauma-related conditions are spiking across every demographic. And modern science has absolutely no framework for addressing any of this.[1,2]

God told me to help correct it, but I thought, *How in the world am I supposed to do that?* To answer, He just kept repeating Himself, "Clean the system." I've been inside the self-development and mindset coaching world since I was young. While I am grateful for the education, I can tell you firsthand that when my life started to fall apart, those methodologies were not sufficient. The self-development world isn't broken by design, but this is what you get when you remove God from the strategy.

In our attempt to build a better future for the next generation, we have accidentally created a scenario where humans are positioned as their own saviors. Not only is this inefficient (we do not possess the processing power to save ourselves, let alone everyone else), but it's also impossible to pull off successfully. All of mankind's attempts to save ourselves have led to cyclical frustration and failure.

For several weeks, I asked God to help me understand what He was asking me to build. I needed the blueprint. Every time I sat down to get instruction, I received more detail. In July of 2025, we beta-launched what He showed me.

I want to be crystal clear about something: the objective of this book is not to position you for a product to purchase. There are far more direct and profitable ways to sell product to the masses. None of them includes rewriting a book four times and laboring over the material. My hope is that this book can be a resource rich enough to study repeatedly, filled with documented accounts of God's promises and His specific commitments to you, personally.

But if you are interested in going deeper, in acquiring more practical and applicable tools that expand beyond just financial success and into every sphere of influence and achievement possible, this is an invitation. In Roman history, a member of "Novos" (literally translated as "new ones") was someone who rose to power despite not coming from an elite family. Novos is not just a brand; it is a threshold. It implies the rise of a new order through a collective of outsiders. It isn't just about change and growth; it is about positioning yourself for ascension.

When a person becomes positioned well, *gravity* shifts around them and they begin to advance without the effort or the grind that traps many in the pursuit of more. The best movements in history are paradoxical… not everyone will understand them, and it's better this way. If everyone understood it, everyone would be living it. I've reached a point in my life and my career where I am no longer willing to build things I am not willing to die for.

Novos is for the ones who've outgrown the noise and want to *shift* themselves into ecosystems of abundance. If you're ready to become the generational linchpin for yourself, your family, and your network, you are invited. More info about Novos Network can be found at novosnetwork.com/currency.

For a list of my projects and social media accounts, visit taylorawelch.com/links. We publish a tremendous amount of free content designed to help you walk out your destiny.

NOTES

DIVINE STRATEGY

1. "Strong's Hebrew: 7389. רֵישׁ (resh or rish) — Poverty, destitution," *Bible Hub*, accessed May 20, 2025, https://biblehub.com/hebrew/7389.htm.
2. Jay W. Richards, *Money, Greed, and God: Why Capitalism Is the Solution and Not the Problem* (New York: HarperOne, 2009).
3. Sendhil Mullainathan and Eldar Shafir, *Scarcity: Why Having Too Little Means So Much* (New York: Macmillan, 2013).
4. Elaine Y. Chou, Bidhan L. Parmar, and Adam D. Galinsky, "Economic Insecurity Increases Physical Pain," *Psychological Science* 27, no. 4 (2016): 443–54, https://doi.org/10.1177/0956797615625644.
5. Walter Mischel, Ebbe B. Ebbesen, and Antonette Raskoff Zeiss, "Cognitive and Attentional Mechanisms in Delay of Gratification," *Journal of Personality and Social Psychology* 21, no. 2 (1972): 204–18.
6. Nathaniel Branden, *The Six Pillars of Self-Esteem* (New York: Bantam Books, 1994).
7. World Bank, "Poverty Headcount Ratio at $1.90 a Day (2011 PPP) (% of Population) - China," *World Bank Data*, 2021.
8. ernando De Soto, *The Mystery of Capital: Why Capitalism Triumphs in the West and Fails Everywhere Else* (New York: Basic Books, 2000).
9. Arvind Panagariya, "India's Trade Reform," in *India Policy Forum 2004*, ed. Stephen Berry, Barry Bosworth, and Arvind Panagariya (Washington, DC: Brookings Institution Press, 2004), 1–57.
10. Michael Sherraden, *Assets and the Poor: A New American Welfare Policy* (Armonk, NY: M.E. Sharpe, 1991).
11. Desen Lin, Shane T. Jensen, and Susan M. Wachter, "The Price Effects of Greening Vacant Lots: How Neighborhood Attributes Matter," *Real Estate Economics*, published online 2023, https://www.researchgate.net/publication/361738963_The_price_effects_of_greening_vacant_lots_How_neighborhood_attributes_matter.
12. William A. Sahlman, "Why Sane People Shouldn't Serve on Public Boards," *Harvard Business Review*, May–June 2020, https://hbr.org/2020/05/why-sane-people-shouldnt-serve-on-public-boards.

GOD WANTS TO FIGHT FOR YOU

1. Keith E. Stanovich, *How to Think Straight About Psychology* (Boston: Pearson Education, 2007).
2. Louis Cozolino, *The Neuroscience of Psychotherapy: Healing the Social Brain*, 3rd ed. (New York: W. W. Norton & Company, 2017).
3. Mary Helen Immordino-Yang and Antonio R. Damasio, "We Feel, Therefore We Learn: The Relevance of Affective and Social Neuroscience to Education," *Mind, Brain, and Education* 1, no. 1 (2007): 3–10.
4. Daniel Goleman, *Emotional Intelligence: Why It Can Matter More Than IQ* (New York: Bantam Books, 1995).

THE GOD OF WAR

1. Richard H. Wilkinson, *The Complete Gods and Goddesses of Ancient Egypt* (New York: Thames & Hudson, 2003).

BELIEF SYSTEMS AND POWER

1. Catharine H. Chatham et al., "Cognitive Control Reflects Context Monitoring, Not Motoric Stopping, in Response Inhibition," *Nature Neuroscience* 14, no. 12 (2011): 1449–53.
2. Malcolm Gladwell, *Blink: The Power of Thinking Without Thinking* (New York: Little, Brown and Company, 2005).
3. Ryan Bush, *Designing the Mind* (City of Publication: Publisher, Year), page number, quoting Joseph E. LeDoux, "Emotion Circuits in the Brain," *Annual Review of Neuroscience* 23, no. 1 (2000): 155–84.
4. Albert Bandura, *Social Learning Theory* (Prentice Hall, 1977).
5. Tim Koller, Marc Goedhart, and David Wessels, *Valuation: Measuring and Managing the Value of Companies* (John Wiley & Sons, 2015).
6. Shalom H. Schwartz, "An Overview of the Schwartz Theory of Basic Values," *Online Readings in Psychology and Culture* 2, no. 1 (2012).
7. Roy F. Baumeister and Stephen J. Scher, "Self-defeating Behavior Patterns among Normal Individuals: Review and Analysis of Common Self-Destructive Tendencies," *Psychological Bulletin* 104, no. 1 (1988): 3–22.
8. Brianna Wiest, *The Mountain Is You: Transforming Self-Sabotage Into Self-Mastery* (Thought Catalog Books, 2020).
9. Roy F. Baumeister and Stephen J. Scher, "Self-Defeating Behavior Patterns Among Normal Individuals: Review and Analysis of Common Self-Destructive Tendencies," *Psychological Bulletin* 104, no. 1 (1988): 3–22.
10. David C. Van Essen et al., "The Human Connectome Project: A Data Acquisition Perspective," *Journal of Neuroscience* 32, no. 45 (2012): 15879–86.

11. Suzana Herculano-Houzel, "The Human Brain in Numbers: A Linearly Scaled-Up Primate Brain," *Frontiers in Human Neuroscience* 3, Article 31 (2009).

12. Edward R. Watkins, "Constructive and Unconstructive Repetitive Thought," *Psychological Bulletin* 134, no. 2 (2008): 163–206.

13. Iain McGilchrist, *The Master and His Emissary: The Divided Brain and the Making of the Western World* (New Haven: Yale University Press, 2009).

14. Howard Eichenbaum, "On the Integration of Space, Time, and Memory," *Neuron* 95, no. 5 (2017): 1007–18.

15. Endel Tulving, "Episodic Memory: From Mind to Brain," *Annual Review of Psychology* 53 (2002): 1–25.

16. Chad J. Marsolek, "Dissociable Neural Subsystems Underlie Abstract and Specific Object Recognition," *Psychological Science* 10, no. 2 (1999): 111–18.

17. Richard J. Davidson and Sharon Begley, *The Emotional Life of Your Brain* (New York: Hudson Street Press, 2012).

18. Alfred Adler, *The Individual Psychology of Alfred Adler: A Systematic Presentation in Selections from His Writings*, ed. Heinz L. Ansbacher and Rowena R. Ansbacher (New York: Basic Books, 1956).

19. Colin M. MacLeod et al., "The Production Effect: Delineation of a Phenomenon," *Journal of Experimental Psychology: Learning, Memory, and Cognition* 36, no. 3 (2010): 671–85.

THE ANATOMY OF FAITH

1. R. R. Reeves et al., "Nocebo Effects with Antidepressant Clinical Drug Trial Placebos," *General Hospital Psychiatry* 29, no. 3 (2007): 275–77.

2. American Psychological Association, "Psychosomatic Pain: When the Mind Creates Real Pain," APA Division of Health Psychology, 2018.

3. Moshe Bar, quoted in David Robson, *The Expectation Effect: How Your Mindset Can Change Your World* (New York: Henry Holt and Company, 2022), publisher's page, accessed October 27, 2025.

THE ALTAR OF GENEROSITY

1. David C. Lindberg, *The Beginnings of Western Science* (Chicago: University of Chicago Press, 1986).

2. John Barton, *The Nature of Biblical Criticism* (Louisville, KY: Westminster John Knox Press, 2007).

3. William Thomson, Lord Kelvin, *Popular Lectures and Addresses* (London: Macmillan and Co., 1891–1894), 1:xxix–xxxii.

4. Genesis 1:26–28

5. Richard P. Feynman, Robert B. Leighton, and Matthew L. Sands, *The*

Feynman Lectures on Physics, vol. 1 (Reading, MA: Addison-Wesley, 1963), 4-1–4-12.

NEXT STEPS

1. Zhang, J., Liu, Q., Liu, J., & Wu, Y. (2025). Trends in prevalent cases and disability-adjusted life years of depressive disorder, 1990–2021: A global burden of disease study. Frontiers in Public Health, 13, 12045679
2. Jones, J. M. (2023, May 17). U.S. depression rates reach new highs. Gallup.

THANK YOU FOR READING MY BOOK!

*I appreciate your interest in my book and value your feedback,
as it helps me improve future versions. I would appreciate it
if you could leave your invaluable review on Amazon.com
with your feedback. Thank you!*